Basketball Math

Slam-Dunk Activities and Projects

Jack A. Coffland and David A. Coffland

GOOD YEAR BOOKS

Pearson Learning Group

Illustrations by Douglas Klauba.

Page abbreviations are as follows:
(C) center, (L) left, (R) right, (BG) background.
      Cover: (BG) Richard Hamilton Smith/Corbis
             (L) Agence France Presse/Corbis
             (R) Reuters NewMedia Inc./Corbis
             (C) Duomo/Corbis

ISBN 0-673-61730-0
Printed in the United States of America
2 3 4 5 6 7 8 9   06 05 04 03 02

1-800-321-3106
www.pearsonlearning.com

Introduction for parents and teachers

When giving students in grades 4–8 problems to solve, we must be certain that they have practiced a wide variety of problems. By the time students are finished at the eighth grade, they should be proficient with problem-solving techniques involving:

- Whole-Number Computation
- Fraction Computation
- Decimal Computation
- Percent Computation

One problem classification system used by many mathematicians includes both "routine" and "nonroutine" problems. In other words, it is no longer appropriate to give students problems that simply review computational operations that have just been taught.

Routine problems

"Routine" problems are defined as those problems that ask students to apply a mathematical process they have learned in class to a real-life, problem-solving situation. This book defines two types of routine problems:

1. Algorithmic problems:

These are word problems (story problems) that ask children to read the problem, figure out the computational procedure required, and then apply that computational algorithm to solve the problem. For example:

Bobby scored 16 points in last night's game. Each shot he made was worth 2 points. How many baskets did he make in all?

2. Multistep problems:

These are algorithmic problems that demand two or more computational steps in order to obtain the answer. For example:

Last year the Bruisers won three-quarters of their 12 games. This year they won 5 games. How many wins did they have over the two seasons?

Similar problems can be made with decimals or percents.

Nonroutine problems

In recent years math educators have focused additional energy on "nonroutine" problems—those that challenge the learner in some way. The different types of nonroutine problems in this book are:

1. Challenge problems:

Problems of this type are nonroutine in that the child does not know how to solve them from memory. They require the use of heuristics, the act of creating a new solution process. It is the true test of problem-solving ability. For example:

Hersey Hawkins scored 1,125 points in his senior season at Drake. He made 87 three-point shots. How many two-point shots did he make? (Hint: He scored 23 more points on free throws than he did on three-pointers.)

Challenge problems appear at the bottom of many of the activity pages.

2. Miniproject problems: Miniproject problems can often be done from one game's statistics. These projects often involve a "process"; they are not simple story problems. They are often open-ended, in that different students may obtain different answers. The process is more important than the product; the process stresses such things as multiple steps, differences in answers, and discussing your considerations to see if everyone agrees. Miniproject problems can often be formed from game statistics. An example is:

How can we interpret and understand a basketball box score? Notice that this task depends upon several variables: not every box score will be the same. Each will have different situations that must be explored. Solving miniproject problems teaches children that not all problems have simple answers, nor do all problems have one answer.

Long-term projects

Finally, since this book is meant to capture the interest of students by combining mathematics and basketball, we have suggested season-long projects. These are not really math problems; they are projects that the student can undertake that require the use of math and a knowledge of basketball. They are meant to be fun and to make math and basketball the child's hobbies.

Problems of this type are the final challenge in math. We cannot quit until we have challenged children to invent or create solutions to problems. The professional scientist, engineer, or mathematician all work to create new ideas, not simply to rehash old ideas. But the myth of mathematics learning has always been that only people in these professions must solve problems. The truth of the situation is that every day the carpenter, the clerical worker, or the grocery store clerk also invents solutions to problems.

Resources

The NCAA issues record books each year for college athletics, listing records for the period of time that the NCAA has been the organizing association for basketball. Examples include:

Official 2000–2001 NCAA Basketball: Records for all Divisions, Men's and Women's Basketball. *NCAA, Indianapolis, Indiana. www.ncaa.org. 1-888-388-9748*

2000–2001 National Collegiate Championships, NCAA, Indianapolis, IN.

The Internet has wonderful statistics. Use a search engine to locate them.

Introduction for students

This book is about basketball; it contains a great deal of interesting information about basketball—professional basketball, men's and women's college basketball, and even high school basketball. But it is also about math. It asks you to solve math problems that stem from basketball statistics, stories, and situations.

The material draws on and attempts to explain key aspects of the game of basketball. For example, you can see how defensive statistics are important. You will be given problems about defensive statistics to figure out for yourself. But you will enjoy the book much more if you also tackle the project on keeping track of defensive statistics for a game or a season. Collect all kinds of statistics on your favorite player; then see if you can figure out how he or she helps the team. Or, if you are playing basketball, keep track of your own statistics and rate yourself!

The book also contains a number of facts and figures about college and professional basketball. For example, who holds the career scoring record for women's college basketball? What college team had the best record over the past ten years? The information is presented in the form of math problems—have fun solving them or give them to your friends to solve. You will already know the answers. Enjoy!

Activities

vii Contents

Projects

ACTIVITIES

Creating a dynasty

The dream of every coach and every team is to have a dynasty—to win several titles quickly. In over fifty years how many NBA teams created a dynasty?

1. The first team to win several titles was the Minneapolis Lakers. From 1949 until 1954, the Lakers won 5 of 6 titles. During that stretch, the team failed to make the finals only once in 1951. How many years ago was the first NBA dynasty created?

_____

2. The Boston Celtics created the longest and most dominant NBA dynasty ever. Boston's first title came in 1957 with Bill Russell playing and Red Auerbach coaching. In the next 13 years they won 11 titles; Bill Russell was a player and coach by then! Boston won 607 regular season games in those years. It failed to win the title only in 1958 and 1967. If Russell was the winning coach for 102 games, how many coaching wins did Auerbach have?

_____

3. Boston and Los Angeles divided eight of the nine titles from 1980 to 1989; Boston won three and Los Angeles won five. Only Philadelphia broke this two-team battle by winning the championship in 1983. Larry Bird led the Celtics and Magic Johnson led the Lakers, with Bird scoring 3,436 playoff points during the eight years and Johnson scoring 2,473 points during the same playoffs. How many more points did Bird score? How many combined points did they have?

_____

4. Michael Jordan and the Chicago Bulls had the latest dynasty. From 1990 to 1998, Michael led the Bulls to six championships over the eight years. (Houston won in 1995 and 1996, when Michael left to play baseball.) Michael scored 529 points during the 1991 playoff games, 759 in the 1992 playoff games, and 666 during the 1993 playoffs. When he returned to the Bulls for the 1995–1996 season, he scored 552 points in the playoffs. He finished his championship run by scoring 590 points and 680 during the playoff games of 1997 and 1998. How many playoff points did Michael Jordan score during Chicago's six championship seasons?

_____

The post-season party

Solve the following problems.

1. In the NBA playoffs, the first round is played using a "best-of-five" format. This means the team that wins three games wins the series. If there are eight first-round playoff series, what is the largest number of games that can be played in the first round?

   _____

2. What is the smallest number of games that can be played in the first round?

   _____

3. After the first round, the playoffs are decided by a "best-of-seven" series. How many games must a team win to clinch a best-of-seven series?

   _____

4. There are eight teams left in the playoffs after the first round. How many series will it take to determine a champion? *(Remember, each series eliminates one team.)*

   _____

5. What is the most number of games that can be played in all of the best-of-seven series?

   _____

6. What is the least number of games that can be played in all of the best-of-seven series?

   _____

7. Using your answers to questions 1, 2, 5, and 6, what are the most and least number of games that can be played in the NBA playoffs?

   _____

March madness

Solve the following problems.

1. Starting in the 2001 NCAA men's tournament, 65 teams participate. Before the first round, two teams from small conferences will play to determine which one will enter the first round. How many games are now played in the first round with 65 teams?

   _____

2. How many games are played in the third round? How many teams participate in this round?

   _____

3. How many rounds does it take to determine a champion?

   _____

Challenge problem

If there are about 370 Division I men's basketball teams, how many rounds would have to be played in order to invite every college to the tournament?

Women's unbeaten teams

The 1986 Texas women's basketball team was the first undefeated team in NCAA women's basketball. The team won 34 games, lost none, and won the women's basketball national championship. Connecticut was the second undefeated team; they had a 35 and 0 record in 1995. Tennessee became the third in 1998, going 39 and 0.

1. The Texas team averaged 83.9 points per game and played 34 games. How many points did they score during the entire season? *(Reasoning question: Should this number be a whole number or a decimal?)*

2. The 1986 Texas women's team had the eighth highest "scoring margin" in NCAA women's basketball history. Now it is the twentieth. *(The scoring margin is the difference between the winning team's score and the losing team's score.)* If the Texas women averaged 83.9 points per game, and their opponents averaged 57.2 points per game, what was the average scoring margin for Texas in 1986?

3. Using the information given in problem 2, how many total points were scored (on the average) during each of the Texas women's team games?

Tennessee 74. How many points were scored in the game?

4. Texas won the national championship in 1986. But during the year, they were ranked second the day they played Tennessee. Who ranked first? Tennessee! The final score when these two teams played was Texas 88,

5. Texas made 1,162 field goals during its 34 games. How many field goals did it make, on the average, during each of those games?

Men's unbeaten teams

Several men's basketball teams have enjoyed undefeated seasons, many of which resulted in a national championship. The following table shows those teams.

Team	Season	Won	Lost
North Carolina	1957	32	0
Indiana	1976	32	0
UCLA	1964	30	0
UCLA	1967	30	0
UCLA	1972	30	0
UCLA	1973	30	0
San Francisco	1956	29	0
North Carolina State	1973	27	0
Kentucky	1954	25	0
LIU-Brooklyn	1939	24	0
Seton Hall	1940	19	0
Army	1944	15	0

1. Obviously, since these teams all went undefeated, they lost no games. How many games were won by all of the teams put together?

2. Some of the undefeated teams did not play in the NCAA championships. During the early years, the NCAA championship was not as popular as it is today. For example, LIU-Brooklyn went undefeated in 1939, but the Oregon Ducks won the first NCAA championship ever played during that year. How many fewer games did the Brooklyn team win in 1939 than the most recent undefeated team—the Indiana Hoosiers?

3. UCLA, during its marvelous winning streak that resulted in ten national championships, had four undefeated teams. How many wins did the Bruins have during all of those undefeated seasons put together?

4. Indiana was the last undefeated men's basketball team. It achieved that honor in 1976.
a. How many years has it been since there was an undefeated team in the NCAA?
b. How many years have passed since the NCAA had its first undefeated team?

The Warriors, state champs

In order to win the state title, the Warriors had to win four straight games at the state tournament. The scores for each game are listed in the following table.

Warriors	83	Wolverines	59
Warriors	58	Comets	52
Warriors	73	Nighthawks	45
Warriors	60	Crusaders	52

1. What was the total number of points scored by the Warriors during the tournament? What was the total for all their opponents combined?

_____

_____

2. What was the average number of points scored by the Warriors? What was the average for all their opponents combined?

_____

_____

3. What was the margin of victory for each game?

_____

_____

4. What was the average margin of victory for the Warriors during the tournament?

_____

_____

Women's scoring champions

Solve the following problems.

1. In both 1992 and 1993 Andrea Congreaves of Mercer led NCAA women's basketball with the highest scoring average. In 1992 she scored 925 points in 28 games. What was her average score per game?

_____

2. In 1993 Andrea's scoring went down, but she still led the nation in scoring. During the 1993 season, she scored 805 points in 26 games. What was her average number of points scored per game that year?

_____

3. Despite Andrea's tremendous scoring in 1992, she does not hold the women's NCAA record for scoring. Patricia Hoskins of Mississippi Valley College earned that distinction. Patricia averaged 33.6 points per game for 27 games in 1989.

How many points did she score during that year? *(Remember this is total points scored, so you have to round off your answer to a whole number.)*

_____

4. Patricia Hoskins also holds the women's NCAA record for most points scored in a career. She scored 3,122 points for Mississipi Valley. Andrea scored only 2,796 points over her entire career at Mercer. How many more points did Patricia score in her entire career? *(Note: During the 2000–2001 season, Jackie Stiles of SW Missouri State was trying to beat this career points record. Did she make it? Yes! Check her new record!)*

_____

The following table shows the top three NCAA women players for total points in a career:

Last year	Name	College	Games	Career points
1989	Patricia Hoskins	Ms. Valley	110	3,122
1984	Lorri Bauman	Drake	120	3,115
1999	Chamique Holdsclaw	Tennessee	148	3,025

5. Who had the highest average for points scored per game? *(Chamique is now an all star player in the WNBA!)*

_____

The Big "O"

Two different basketball players have led the NCAA in scoring average for three years—Oscar Robinson of Cincinnati and Pete Maravich of Louisiana State. Both went on to have long careers in the NBA. The following chart shows Oscar Robinson's NCAA career statistics.

Oscar Robinson—6 ft., 5 in. guard

Year	Games	Field goals	Free throws	Total points	Game average
1958	28	352	280	984	35.1
1959	30	331	316	978	32.6
1960	30	369	273	1011	33.7

1. How many field goals did Oscar Robinson make in his NCAA career?

_____

2. How many total points did Robinson score in the three seasons he played for Cincinnati? *(He ranks 7th on the all-time list of career scorers.)*

_____

3. How many free throws did Robinson make in his NCAA career?

_____

Challenge problem

Can you figure Robinson's average points over his entire NCAA career? Be careful; you can't use the game averages given in the table to calculate this. Do you know why?

Pearson Education, Inc./Good Year Books, Basketball Math. All rights reserved.

"Pistol" Pete

Two different basketball players have led the NCAA in scoring average for three years—Oscar Robinson of Cincinnati and Pete Maravich of Louisiana State. Both went on to have long careers in the National Basketball Association. The following chart shows Pistol Pete Maravich's NCAA career statistics.

Year	Games	Field goals	Free throws	Total points	Game average
1968	26	432	274	1,138	43.8
1969	26	433	282	1,148	44.2
1970	31	522*	337	1,381*	44.5*

* Indicates record

2. How many total points did Pistol Pete score in the three seasons he played for LSU? *(That number ranks Maravich first in NCAA "career points"—the statistical category for total points scored in a career.)*

_____

3. How many free throws did Maravich make in his NCAA career?

_____

Challenge problem

Pistol Pete was criticized at times for shooting too much. Do you think points scored is the only statistic that is important? What other statistic might also be important when considering how many points a player scored?

1. How many field goals did Maravich make in his NCAA career?

_____

Point guards

One way to rate the effectiveness of a point guard is to calculate the assist/turnover ratio. The ratio is found by dividing the number of assists by the number of turnovers. If the point guard has a ratio larger than 1:1, then he or she is considered to be doing a good job.

Player	Assists	Turnovers	Ratio
Jason	27	12	:
Jeremy	30		2.5:1
Fred		40	1.5:1
Efrain	128	80	:

1. What is Jason's assist/turnover ratio?

_____

2. How many turnovers did Jeremy commit during the season?

_____

3. How many assists did Fred have for the season?

_____

4. What was Efrain's ratio of assists to turnovers?

_____

5. Which one of the players do you think started for the team? How did you choose your answer?

_____

Women's field-goal percentage leaders

Scoring in basketball is an interesting problem. A player wants to score, but does not like to miss a shot. So, an interesting statistic is called "field-goal percentage." It tells the percent of shots that a player makes. Obviously, a player would like to score a lot of points and take very few shots. But some scorers take and miss a large number of shots. There is a point when a player is not helping his or her team if too many shots are missed.

The following table shows the six highest field-goal percentages in women's college basketball for an entire season. Obviously, these are very good shooters; they don't miss many! Can you complete the table? Remember, for example, that no player can take a half shot, so the number of field goals must come out to be a whole number. A field goal percentage, on the other hand, should be computed to one decimal place.

Name/College	Season	Games	Field goals	Attempts	Percent
Myndee Larsen, S. Utah	1998	28	—	344	72.4
Deneka Knowles, SE Louisiana	1996	26	199	—	72.1
Barbara Farris, Tulane	1998	27	151	210	–.–
Renay Adams, Tenn. Tech	1991	30	—	258	71.7
Regina Days, Ga. Southern	1986	27	234	—	70.5
Kim Woods, Wisconsin, GB	1994	27	188	271	–.–

Comparing field-goal percentages

The "field-goal percentage" statistic is important when you compare how making and missing a shot will help a team. Examine the statistical lines for two players.

Player	Field goals made	Field goals attempted	Shooting percent	3 FG made	3 FG attempted	3 point %
Angie	282	670	42.1	2	9	22.2
Becky	272	421	64.6	1	4	25.0

Compare these two players. Angie scored more points, but:

1. How many times did Angie shoot the ball and miss?

_____

2. If you assume a two-point field goal for each Angie miss, how many points did she cost her team?

_____

3. How many times did Becky shoot the ball and miss?

_____

4. If you assume a two-point field goal for each Becky miss, how many points did she cost her team?

_____

Challenge problem

Figure the total points scored by each player. Then: Angie shot the ball a total of 670 times that her team had the ball. Becky shot the ball a total of 421 times her team had the ball. How many points were scored, on the average, for each time the player shot? (Remember, three-pointers are included in the total number of shots taken.)

UCLA's championships

The UCLA Bruins, under coach John Wooden, had an unbelievable string of national championships. No one has ever come close to UCLA's record. The following numbers show how fantastic the record is.

Year	Champion	Score	Second	Third	Fourth
1964	UCLA	98–83	Duke	Michigan	Kansas State
1965	UCLA	91–80	Michigan	Princeton	Wichita State
1966	UTEP	72–65	Kentucky	Duke	Utah
1967	UCLA	79–64	Dayton	Houston	N. Carolina
1968	UCLA	78–55	N. Carolina	Ohio State	Houston
1969	UCLA	92–72	Purdue	Drake	N. Carolina
1970	UCLA	80–69	Jacksonville	New Mexico State	St. Bonaventure
1971	UCLA	68–62	Villanova	Western Kentucky	Kansas
1972	UCLA	81–76	Florida State	N. Carolina	Louisville
1973	UCLA	87–66	Memphis State	Indiana	Providence
1974	N. Car. St.	76–64	Marquette	UCLA	Kansas
1975	UCLA	92–85	Kentucky	Louisville	Syracuse
1976	Indiana	86–68	Michigan	UCLA	Rutgers

1. How many years are covered in the chart above? _____

During this period of time:

2. How many first-place finishes did UCLA have? _____

3. How many third-place finishes did UCLA have? _____

4. How many times did UCLA fail to make the Final Four? _____

5. What was UCLA's average score   during its championship games? _____

6. What was the second-place team's average score against UCLA?

_____

Duke's championships

The only team who has even thought about returning to the Final Four several times in recent years has been the Duke Blue Devils. Their record for Final Four appearances in recent years is listed below. If you compare Duke's streak to UCLA's on page 14 you will see how truly fantastic the UCLA streak was. Why? Because Duke's Coach Mike Krzyzewski, known as Coach "K," is considered to have done quite well to have made the Final Four as many times as he did. Answer the following questions to examine Duke's string of appearances. They won again in 2001.

Year	Champion	Score	Second	Third*
1986	Louisville	72–69	Duke	Kansas and Louisiana State
1987	Indiana	74–73	Syracuse	Nevada–LV and Providence
1988	Kansas	83–79	Oklahoma	Arizona and Duke
1989	Michigan	80–79	Seton Hall	Duke and Illinois
1990	Nevada–Las Vegas	103–73	Duke	Arkansas and Georgia Tech
1991	Duke	72–65	Kansas	Nevada–LV and North Carolina
1992	Duke	71–51	Michigan	Cincinnati and Indiana
1993	North Carolina	77–71	Michigan	Kansas and Kentucky
1994	Arkansas	76–72	Duke	Arizona and Florida

* After 1981, no third place game is played

1. How many years are covered in the chart above?

_____

2. How many first-place finishes did Duke have during this time?

_____

3. How many second-place finishes did Duke have during this time?

_____

4. How many times was Duke tied for third during this period?

_____

5. How many times did Duke fail to make the Final Four during this period?

_____

6. What was Duke's average score during its championship games? (Don't forget Duke losses!)

_____

NCAA women's championships

The NCAA took over women's basketball in the early 1980s, holding the first women's Final Four in 1982. The record of NCAA Division 1 college championships from 1990 to 2000 is shown in the table below.

Year	Champion	Score	Second	Winning coach
1990	Stanford	88–81	Auburn	Tara VanDerveer
1991	Tennessee	70–67	Virginia	Pat Summitt
1992	Stanford	78–62	Western Ky	Tara VanDerveer
1993	Texas Tech	84–82	Ohio State	Marsha Sharp
1994	North Carolina	60–59	Louisiana Tech	Sylvia Hatchell
1995	Connecticut	70–64	Tennessee	Geno Auriemma
1996	Tennessee	83–65	Georgia	Pat Summitt
1997	Tennessee	68–59	Old Dominion	Pat Summitt
1998	Tennessee	93–75	Louisiana Tech	Pat Summitt
1999	Purdue	62–45	Duke	Carolyn Peck
2000	Connecticut	71–45	Tennessee	Geno Auriemma

What information can you summarize from this table? Consider the following questions:

1. Tennessee has four championships. Figure:

    a. its average score in those victories

    b. its opponent's average score

    c. the average margin of victory

2. Connecticut and Stanford both won two championships in this time period. For each team, figure:

    a. its average score in those victories

3. Louisiana Tech and Tennessee both finished second two times in the time period 1990-2000. That must have been difficult for the players to accept. They came so close, but they did not win the championships. What was Tennessee's average margin of defeat? What was Louisiana Tech's average margin of defeat?

4. Which teams have won only one championship?

Sheryl Swoopes, 1993 MVP

During the 1993 Women's Basketball Division I Championship, Sheryl Swoopes from Texas Tech led her team to its first-ever national championship. Sheryl had the kind of tournament that most people only dream about. She led all players in eight different offensive categories; she was named as the unanimous choice for the Women's Final Four Most Outstanding Player. Examine her statistics to see what kind of a tournament she had.

As you can see, Sheryl led the tournament in eight categories. She also scored 47 points in the championship game *(a championship game record)*, which Texas Tech won by a score of 84–82 over Ohio State. Obviously, Sheryl is a true champion. But to see how fantastic her tournament actually was, compute the rest of her statistics.

Games	5	Assists	11
Field goals	56*	Free throws	57*
Field goals attempted	110*	FT attempted	*
Field-goal percent		FT percent	93.4%
Rebounds	48*	Total points	177*
Rebounds per game		Game average	*
* = a record			

1. What was Sheryl's field-goal shooting percentage?

_____

2. How many free throws did Sheryl attempt? *(Remember, your answer must be rounded to a whole number; she can't shoot half a free throw.)*

_____

3. How many rebounds did Sheryl average for each game?

_____

4. How many points did Sheryl average for each game?

_____

Challenge problem

Sheryl made some three-point shots as well. How many?

_____

Hiding the three-point shots

Statistics can hide in a chart. Take a look, for example, at those in the following chart.

Selected top 10 single game-scoring performances in an NCAA women's tournament game				
Player/Institution vs. Opponent/Year	Round	FG	FT	Points
Lorri Bauman, Drake vs. Maryland, 1982	RC	21	8	50
Sheryl Swoopes, Texas Tech vs. Ohio State, 1993	C	16	11	47
Chamique Holdsclaw, Tenn. vs. Boston C., 1999	2nd	15	19	49
Kerry Bascom, Conn. vs. Toledo, 1991	2nd	13	8	39
Shannon Cate, Montana vs. Iowa, 1991	1st	16	2	36
Sheryl Swoopes, Texas Tech vs. Colorado, 1993	RC	10	15	36

Key: 1st=First Round, 2nd=Second Round, RC=Regional Championship, C=National Championship Game

What statistic is hiding here? The NCAA reports only field goals in this statistic; it does not reveal how many three-point shots the individual made. But if you compute the total points from the individual basket scores, you find that counting every field goal as a two-point basket and then adding in the free throws does not equal the total number of points. Therefore, some of the players listed above must have made three-point shots. How many? You figure it out. *(Hint: Some players did not make any.)*

Three-point baskets

Three-point baskets *Hint: Some players did not make any*

Lorri Bauman   = _____

Sheryl Swoopes   = _____
(Ch. Game)

Chamique
Holdsclaw   = _____

Kerry Bascom   = _____

Shannon Cate   = _____

Sheryl Swoopes   = _____

Mom's challenge problems

"Hey Karen," Mom shouted. "I've made up some brain teasers from Prescott's basketball games over the weekend. Do you want to try to solve them?"

"Sure," Karen replied. "Let's have them."

Here are the brain teasers for Karen—can you solve them?

1. Sade made the exact same number of free throws, two-point shots, and three-point shots. If she scored 30 points altogether in Friday's game, how many points did she score on three-point shots?

2. Loni scored 35 points in Saturday's game. She did not make any three-point shots, and she hit twice as many field goals as free throws. How many field goals and free throws did she make?

3. During Friday's game, Prescott scored 10 more than twice as many points as Sade scored. How many did Prescott score?

Charity stripe stories

Free throws are taken when a player is fouled. For some, the shot is a reward. For others, it's like a punishment. Consider the following free-throw records.

Player	Year	FTM	FTA	Percent made
Calvin Murphy	1981	206	215	
Shaquille O'Neal*	2000	135	296	
Reggie Miller	2000	373	406	
Chris Dudley	1990	58	182	
Karl Malone	1986	195	405	
Karl Malone	2000	589	739	

*Shaq's statistics are for the 23 Laker playoff games only!
Key: FTM=free throws made, FTA=free throws attempted

1. Calvin Murphy holds the single-season record for the highest percentage of free throws made in one year. He set the record in 1981. What was his FTM percentage during that record year? Fill in the space in the table.

_____

2. Shaquille O'Neal often has free-throw problems. His team—the Lakers—won the 2000 league championship and O'Neal was named the "Most Valuable Player." But opponents tried to beat the Lakers by fouling O'Neal at the end of a game—the "Hack-a-Shaq" strategy. Teams like Portland hoped to beat the Lakers if Shaq missed free throws. Compute Shaq's FTM percentage for the playoffs to see why.

_____

3. Reggie Miller is one of the best free-throw shooters playing today. What was his FTM percentage during the 1999–2000 season?

_____

4. Chris Dudley, a center (teams—Cleveland, New Jersey, Portland, and New York), is one of the worst free-throw shooters ever. His worst year for shooting free throws occurred in 1989–1990 when he played for Cleveland and New Jersey. What was his FTM percentage during that year?

_____

5. Karl Malone's record is interesting. He could be a role model for O'Neal and Dudley. Karl was a terrible free-throw shooter in 1986, his first year. But he improved steadily. The 1999–2000 season was his best ever. Find his FTM percentage for both years, then figure his percentage improvement over the 14 years.

_____

NBA record holders

The most cherished record for an NBA player is the "career record" for a category. That honor goes only to players who play very well for many years. Players who hold career records are special! An example: Kareem Abdul Jabbar, one of the NBA's greatest centers, holds a number of career records.

All-time scoring leader

Kareem Abdul Jabbar scored more points than anyone else in the NBA. Kareem came into the NBA in 1969 and played 20 seasons. During that time, he scored 38,387 points. (Did you know that he originally played for the Milwaukee Bucks as Lew Alcindor? He later changed his team and his name!) For his entire career, then, how many points did he average per year? *(Note: Kareem had amazing health; he missed only 80 games during the 20 regular seasons.)*

All-time shot leader

Kareem also holds the career record for "most field goals attempted" and "most field goals made." He attempted 28,307 shots and made 15,837 of them. First, get a calculator and figure his shooting percentage (shots made divided by total shots). Over his entire career he made over 50% of his shots! On the other hand, he made only 1 of 18 three-point shots. What was his three-point shooting percentage? (This would hardly qualify for a record!)

All-time playing leader

Kareem also holds the record for career minutes played. He spent more time on the NBA court than any other player. His record is 57,446 minutes played. Robert Parrish holds the record for most seasons played in the NBA. During his record 21 years in the NBA, he played 45,704 minutes. How many more minutes did Kareem play?

Hot shots

Carrie and Anji are racing for the scoring title in their teams' conference. With one week to go in the season, their statistics look like this:

Player	Games	Points	Average	Games left
Carrie	18		16.0	2
Anji	19	305		1

Complete the table, then answer the following questions.

1. Who has the higher average at this point in the season?

_____

2. Who has scored the most points so far?

_____

3. Carrie then scores 14 points in her next game. Is she ahead of Anji's total?

_____

4. Anji scores 20 points in the final game of her season. What will be her point average per game for the whole season?

_____

5. How many points will Carrie need to score in her last game to win the scoring title?

_____

Shooting for the perimeter

When the painter gets ready to paint the court for a professional basketball team, he must use the diagram below to plan the job. The painter knows that he will have to put masking tape down before he paints each part of the court. He does this to prevent the workers from accidentally changing the lengths of the lines. In the following problems, assume that the painter puts tape on one side of each line.

Basketball court dimensions

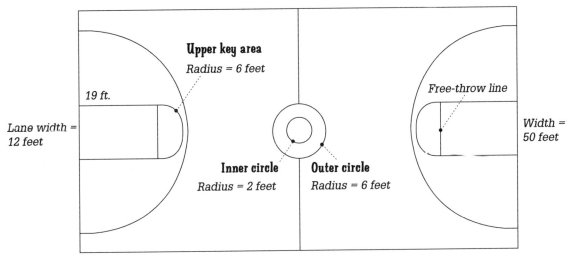

Upper key area
Radius = 6 feet

19 ft.

Free-throw line

*Lane width =
12 feet*

Inner circle
Radius = 2 feet

Outer circle
Radius = 6 feet

*Width =
50 feet*

Length = 94 feet

1. How much tape will the painter need to go around the entire court?

_____

2. If the painter has already painted the perimeter of the court, he won't need to repaint the part of the lane that is on the baseline. How much tape will he need to finish both sides of the lane and the free-throw line at one end of the court?

_____

Challenge problems

What is the perimeter of the lane, including the semicircular area behind the free-throw line?

After the painter finishes painting the outer jump circle at the center of the floor, he wonders what the total length is around the edge of that circle. What is this length? (*Hint: It is called the circumference.*)

Covering the area

After painting all of the lines on the basketball court, the painter
has to paint some sections of the floor in the team colors. The
areas that usually get painted are the lanes and the jump circle.
(Refer to the diagram on page 23.)

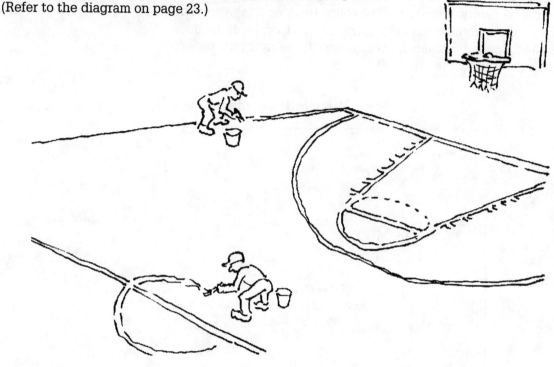

1. How many square feet will be
painted in the lane on each end of
the court? How much area will be
covered in both lanes combined?
(*Note: The circular area behind the
free-throw line is not part of
the "lane."*)

_____

_____

2. How many square feet are painted in
the jump circle (*the outer circle*) at
mid-court?

_____

3. At the top of each lane, there is a half
circle from which foul shots are taken.
What is the area of one of these half-
circles? What is the combined area of
both of the half-circles?

_____

_____

4. After all of the painting is done, the
painter must finish the job by
applying a coat of varnish to the
entire floor. What is the total area
covered by the varnish?

_____

_____

Famous duos

Two famous players on the same team are often paired together to the point where it is difficult to think of one without the other. Examine the following problems to discover some interesting facts about four famous duos!

1. What famous player pair has played together for the longest time? John Stockton and Karl Malone are one possibility. Stockton's NBA career began in 1984 and Malone's in 1985. They've played together ever since! Stockton held the career-assist record at the start of the 2000–2001 season with 13,780 assists. Malone entered the 2000–2001 season in third place on the list of all-time scoring leaders with 31,041 points and during the year moved into second place. Stockton played 16 seasons to establish the assist mark shown above, and Malone played 15 seasons to establish his point total. So, what is the average number of assists per season for Stockton and the average number of points per season for Malone?

2. What famous pair of very tall players led the San Antonio Spurs to the NBA championship in 1999? The Twin Towers—David Robinson and Tim Duncan! If Duncan scored 1,084 points during that year, and if Robinson scored 775 points that year, then how many more points did Tim Duncan score? (Note: These point totals are low because a strike shortened the season to 50 games that year.)

3. What famous pair led their team to the most NBA championships recently? Michael Jordan and Scottie Pippin led the Bulls to six NBA championships during the 1990's. Scottie's best year for total points was in 1991–1992 when he scored 1,720. Michael's best year for total points in a championship season was in 1990–1991 when he scored 2,580. How many points did they score when you combine their best point totals in a championship season? (Note: Jordan scored 3,041 points in 1986–1987, but the Bulls did not win the championship that year.)

4. What pair became famous competing against each other? Larry Bird and Magic Johnson seemed to be playing against each other for the NBA championships during most of the 1980's. Magic's highest scoring total was 1,909 points in 1986–1987. Bird's highest single-season scoring effort was 2,295 in 1984–1985. How many more points did Larry score in his best season than Magic?

The NBA all-star team, 1999–2000

The following chart shows the NBA all-star team for the 1999–2000 season, along with the games played and the total number of points scored for each of the all-stars. Refer to the chart to answer the questions below.

First Team				Second Team		
Player	Games	Points		Player	Games	Points
Kevin Garnett	81	1,857		Grant Hill	74	1,906
Tim Duncan	74	1,716		Karl Malone	82	2,095
Shaq O'Neal	79	2,344		Alonzo Mourning	79	1,718
Gary Payton	82	1,982		Allan Iverson	70	1,989
Jason Kidd	67	959		Kobe Bryant	66	1,485

1. Which team scored more total points, the first or second all-star team?

_____

2. Compute the points per game for each player. (*Note: Each had a different number of games, usually because of injuries. Therefore, you have to divide each player's total points by the number of games actually played.*)

_____

Read and compute

The normal NBA season includes 82 games. Who played in all of their team's games? Who played in the least number of games? How many games did each player miss? What was the difference between most games played and least games played?

_____

Thinking question

Do you suppose a player would be named an all star if he played in only 10 or 15 games during the year? Why or why not?

_____

3. Some second-team players scored more than first-team players. Since the players are paired by position, you can compare them directly across. Which second-team all-star scored more points than the first-team all-star? Who had the greatest point difference? Figure this out for total points and points per game.

_____

Shot blockers

Defensive statistics are becoming more important as people begin to understand the importance of playing strong defense. Consider the following chart showing the leading college women's shot blockers for several years.

Year	Player/Team	Games	Blocks	Average
1989	Michelle Wilson/Texas South	27	151	_._*
1990	Simone Srubek, Fresno State	31	138	4.5
1991	Suzanne Johnson, Monmouth	23	117	5.1
1992	Denise Hogue, Charleston	28	147	5.3
1993	Chris Enger, San Diego	28	_	4.9
1994	Rebecca Lobo, Connecticut	33	131	4.0

*= record

1. Consider what these statistics mean to their respective teams. Most shots are blocked close to the basket where the shooting percentages are very high. If all of the shots that Rebecca Lobo blocked had been good, how many more total points would Connecticut's opponents have scored? (*Note: Rebecca went on to the WNBA.*)

_____

2. In that same manner, if all of the shots that Suzanne Johnson blocked had been good, how many more points would Monmouth's opponents have scored each game?

_____

3. Michelle Wilson holds the record for "most blocked shots per game, average." What is her record? (*Carry your answer out to one decimal point; that is the way the NCAA keeps its records.*)

_____

4. How many shots did Chris Enger block for San Diego in 1993? (*Remember, you can't block half a shot; round off your answer to the nearest whole number.*)

_____

Wanted for stealing

Another defensive statistic is the "steal" category. This implies that a defensive player on one team steals the ball before the other team can shoot. Natalie White of Florida A&M holds several women's records for stealing the ball from the opponent. Consider her records.

Most Steals in a Game: 14, by Natalie White of Florida A&M vs. South Alabama on December 13,1991 *(now tied with four others)*.

Most Steals in a Season: Natalie White—191 steals in a 30-game season during 1995. In fact, Natalie also holds the second-best season record, with 172 steals in 28 games during 1994.

1. Consider what Natalie's steals meant to her team when they played South Alabama back in 1991. Then answer the following questions:

a. Largest possible points prevented: Assume that South Alabama would have made three-point shots on every possession *(14)* where Natalie stole the ball. How many points did she prevent?

_____

b. More probable: If South Alabama had made two-point shots on every possession where Natalie stole the ball, how many points did she prevent?

_____

c. Most probable: Assume South Alabama would make half of its shots (all two-pointers) on the possessions where Natalie stole the ball. How many points did Natalie prevent?

_____

2. Natalie's season record of 191 steals was made in 1995. Assume the "most probable" situation *(described above)*: If her opponents had kept the ball and made half of the shots, how many points did Natalie prevent the opponents from scoring during the entire season of 1995?

_____

Reasoning question

Assume that a team wins a game by the score of 65 to 63 and one of its players steals the ball seven times. Do you think the player had an impact upon the final score? Why or why not?

Very famous players doing other things

Every basketball fan remembers Magic and Larry; people who don't even like basketball know Michael. Here are little known facts about these players.

1. Magic Johnson delighted basketball fans for years. He led Michigan State to the NCAA championship and the Los Angeles Lakers to NBA championships. But did you know he also coached the Lakers for part of a season? As a coach, Magic's team won 5 games and lost 11. Can you compute his winning percentage for coaching? (Hint: As a player, he did better.)

2. Larry Bird played against Magic for years. Bird's Indiana State team lost to Johnson's team in the NCAA championship game, but Bird's Boston Celtics won NBA championships against Magic's Lakers. Bird was a fantastic player but did you know that he also coached an NBA team?

Larry coached the Indianapolis Pacers for three years, taking them to the NBA finals in 2000. (The Pacers lost to the Lakers in six games.) Larry's coaching record is:

Find Larry's total number of wins and losses as a coach. Then compute his regular season winning percentage, his playoff winning percentage, and his total winning percentage.

3. Michael Jordan never coached in the NBA but he became general manager of the Washington Wizards in 2000. Mike has his work to do; he could probably help the Wizards by playing. In January 2001, during Michael's first whole season as GM, the Wizards lost five times as many games as they won. If they won only five games, can you figure how many losses they had, how many total games they played, and what their winning percentage was? (Hint: It wasn't very good; the team was last in its division.)

| | Regular Season | | Playoff Record | |
Year	Wins	Losses	Wins	Losses
97–98	58	24	10	6
98–99	33	17	9	4
99–00	56	26	13	10

Play like Mike

Michael Jordan is regarded as the best basketball player of all time if not the best athlete of all time. As a result, every new NBA player with promise is eventually compared to Jordan—to see if they can "play like Mike." Use the following chart to answer the questions below.

Michael Jordan's statistics for his first four NBA seasons

Year	Minutes	FGM	FGA	%	FTM	FTA	%	Total points	Points games
1	3144	837	1625	51.5	630	746	84.5	2313	28.2
2	451	150	328	45.7	105	125	84.0	408	22.7
3	3281	1098	2279	48.2	833	972	85.7	3041	37.1
4	3311	1069	1998	53.5	733	860	84.1	2868	35.0

1. How many more points did Michael score in his first year in the NBA than in his second year?

_____

2. The statistics obviously show that Michael Jordan didn't do much in his second year. The reason is that he played in only 18 games. If he played 451 minutes in 18 games, how many minutes per game did he play on the average?

_____

3. What is the difference between Michael's highest total points figure for his first four years and his lowest?

_____

Son of play like Mike

Kobe Bryant is the latest talented young player to be compared to Michael Jordan. Kobe is about the same size and plays the same position. So, why not compare him to Michael? Let's compare the first four years of Jordan's career with the first four years of Bryant's career in the NBA. The following table shows the basic statistics for Kobe Bryant during his first four years in the NBA. Use Jordan's statistics from page 30 to make your comparison.

Kobe Bryant's statistics for his first four NBA seasons

Year	Minutes	FGM	FGA	%	FTM	FTA	%	Total points	Points games
1	1103	176	422	42.7	136	166	81.9	539	7.6
2	2056	391	913	42.8	363	457	79.4	1220	15.2
3	1896	362	779	46.5	234	292	83.9	996	19.9
4	2524	554	1183	46.8	331	403	82.1	1485	22.5

1. How many more points did Michael score in his first year than Kobe?

_____

2. How many more minutes did Michael play in his first year than Kobe?

_____

Common-sense questions

Why do you suppose that Kobe played so much less than Michael when comparing first year playing time?

Why do you suppose that Michael played in only 18 games during his second year in the league?

_____

3. Mike's highest points per game for the statistics shown came in his third year, while Kobe's came in his fourth. How many more points per game did Michael have when you compare these two years?

_____

Final thought

What do you think? Is it fair to compare Kobe to Michael? At the beginning of his career? Today? In the future?

_____

Do you really want to hold this record?

Not every record is something a player would like to hold. Consider the following questionable records.

Quickest disqualification ever

Anyone can have a bad day. But sometimes "bad" is really bad. On December 29, 1997, Bubba Wells of the Dallas Mavericks fouled out of a game after playing only three minutes. In other words, he collected 6 fouls in three minutes. Figure a ratio for this. If Wells was allowed to play all 48 minutes and he continued to foul at the same rate, how many fouls would he commit in the entire game?

All-time leader in turnovers

Players have to be very good to set some questionable records. Why? To hold a negative *career* record, you have to play. And you have to play a long time. You can't set the record if you're sitting on the bench!

What player turned the ball over more than anyone? This player is the one who lost the ball to the opposing team more times than anyone else. Moses Malone is that player. In 19 seasons Malone committed 3,804 turnovers. On the average, how many turnovers did he commit in a season? *(Note: Moses only led the league in turnovers one year—1980–1981.)*

Most fouls in one game

Who holds the record for most fouls in one game? Don Otten, playing in the NBA's first year, committed 8 fouls in one game. The game was held on November 24, 1949 between the Tri-Cities and Sheboygan teams. (Have you ever heard of these NBA teams?) Since a player now leaves the game after six fouls, this is a record to question!

Research project

Can you find an old newspaper in the library to see how this record occurred?

Amazing championship stories

The NCAA keeps detailed records for the championship playoffs. Each year 64 teams are selected to take part in the playoffs; over the years some truly amazing things have happened, and some great basketball players have been a part of the action. Consider the following stories.

1. Christian Laettner of Duke is the coholder of the highest field goal percentage figure for one game; he shot 100%—ten shots taken, ten made—during Duke's 104–103 win over Kentucky in the regional final game in 1992. What is truly amazing was Laettner's last shot. Kentucky was ahead; Duke had time only to catch the in-bounds pass and shoot. But Laettner grabbed the pass, turned, and shot all in one motion. The shot, his tenth of the game, was perfect. Laettner scored, Kentucky lost, and Duke went on to win the national championship. What was the total number of points scored in this exciting game?

2. North Carolina won the national championship in 1982, when both Michael Jordan and James Worthy played for the Tarheels. Even with these two great players, the Tarheels were locked in a tight battle with Georgetown in the championship game. It was a close contest, but with seconds left, North Carolina went ahead of Georgetown by one point, 63 to 62. Now the Tarheels had only to keep Georgetown from scoring. Georgetown brought the ball down court. The pressure was tight. The Georgetown guard turned and passed the ball backwards to a wide-open player. But it was not his teammate—it was James Worthy of North Carolina. Astonished, Worthy caught the ball and dribbled toward his basket. Time expired. North Carolina had won. Georgetown was distraught. But for one bad pass, the Hoyas might have been the national champions. How many total points were scored in this game?

Three famous college shot blockers

Three very famous NBA centers hold all of the blocked shot records in the NCAA playoffs. None of the famous centers, however, could lead his team to the NCAA championship. Who are they? Read on and solve these story problems.

2. David Robinson holds the record for most blocked shots during one championship series. In 1986, his Navy team played four games before being eliminated. During those four games the "Admiral" blocked 23 shots. What was his blocked-shot average for each of the four games?

3. Alonzo Mourning holds the record for most blocked shots during a career. His Georgetown team made the NCAA playoffs every year from 1989 through 1992. During that time, he played in 10 games and blocked 37 shots. If he could do this over an entire 28-game season, how many shots would "Lo" block over the season?

Challenge problem

Two of these questions ask you to compute what a season's worth of shot blocks would be based upon a few games. What is wrong with using this reasoning to assume what the season record might be?

1. Shaquille O'Neal, the "Shaq," holds the NCAA championship series record for most blocked shots in one game. Louisiana State was playing Brigham Young in the first round of the 1992 playoffs. Brigham Young had several good big men, but Shaq was the master of the paint. He blocked 11 shots in one game. If Shaq could have done this every game for a 28-game season, how many shots would he have blocked over the entire season?

Senator Bradley's records

Some young people may not realize that former Senator Bill
Bradley of New Jersey was at one time a star basketball player
with the Princeton Tigers and the New York Knicks. In fact,
Bradley still holds some NCAA playoff records. Read the
following problems to learn more about these records.

1. Bill Bradley of Princeton is tied with a
player from Wyoming named Fennis
Dembo for having the highest free-
throw percentage in one game. Both
made 16 out of 16 free throws during
a playoff game—Bradley against St.
Joseph's in the first round of 1963 and
Dembo against UCLA in the second
round of 1987. How many years
passed between these two record
performances?

2. Bradley also held the career record
for highest free-throw percentage
during the NCAA playoffs until 1999
when it was broken by Authur Lee of
Stanford (58-62). Bradley's Princeton
team was invited to the playoffs
three years in a row, from 1963
through 1965. During that time, he
made 87 out of 96 free-throw shots.
To qualify for this record, a player
must have attempted a minimum of
50 free throws. By how many
attempts is Bradley over the
minimum?

Challenge problem

A career record like Bradley's free-throw record carries with it a
minimum number of tries. Why do you think this is the case? Do
you see how a record might be worthless without the minimum
number of tries requirement?

The long and the short of it

In the 2000–2001 season, the New York Knicks' roster looked like this:

Player	Height	Weight
Camby	6'11"	225 lbs.
Childs	6'3"	195 lbs.
Houston	6'6"	200 lbs.
Johnson	6'7"	235 lbs.
Knight	7'0"	235 lbs.
Longley	7'2"	260 lbs.
Postell	6'6"	212 lbs.
Rice	6'8"	220 lbs.
Sprewell	6'5"	190 lbs.
Strickland	6'3"	210 lbs.
Thomas	6'9"	230 lbs.
Ward	6'2"	190 lbs.

1. If the coach decided to put the five tallest players on the floor at once, who would they be?

_____

2. How many total inches would that team add up to?

_____

3. What would be the total height of the shortest team the coach could put on the floor?

_____

4. What is the difference in height (in inches) between the tallest player and the shortest player on the team? (This number is called the "range in height.")

_____

5. What is the average weight of the Knicks?

_____

6. What is the range of weight for the team?

_____

7. What are the total weights of the heaviest and lightest teams that the coach could put on the floor?

_____

8. Is the lightest team composed of the same five players as the shortest?

_____

All-time records

All-time steal leader

Everyone knows John Stockton holds the career record for most assists. (He was still playing when this book was written, adding to his record every game! See *Famous Duos* on page 25 for that record.) But as the 2000–2001 season began, he also held the record for most career steals. He played 16 seasons at that time, averaging 177.75 steals per season. What was Stockton's most career steals record at the beginning of the 2000–2001 season?

_____

Who's doing it now?

Seattle star Gary Payton is famous for his defense. He guards players so tightly he is called "the Glove." At the beginning of the 2000–2001 season, Payton had 1,756 steals and had played for 10 seasons. How many steals did he average each year?

_____

All-time rebounding leader

Wilt Chamberlain holds the career record for most rebounds. He collected 23,924 rebounds during the 14 regular seasons that he played. On the average, how many rebounds did Wilt have each year?

_____

Who's doing it now?

Recently, Dennis Rodman was known as an excellent rebounder. He collected a total of 11,954 rebounds during his 14 regular seasons. How many more rebounds did Wilt grab than Rodman?

_____

Calculator problem

Even though both players spent 14 years in the league, Wilt played 47,859 minutes compared to 28,839 minutes for Rodman. With a calculator, figure out who got the most rebounds per minute.

_____

Two famous Malones

It is interesting to compare the statistics of two famous NBA players with the same last name: Moses Malone and Karl Malone. *(A research question: There are other famous NBA players named Malone. Can you find one?)*

Interesting comparison

Karl Malone played his entire career as a power forward for one team—the Utah Jazz. Moses, on the other hand, played center for several teams. He started his career in the American Basketball Association (ABA) with the Utah Stars and moved to the St. Louis Spirits. After the ABA and NBA merger, Moses played for Buffalo, Houston, Philadelphia, and San Antonio. That's a lot of teams.

Some career statistics

Player	Years	Games	Minutes	Points	Rebounds
Karl	15	1,192	44,608	31,041	12,618
Moses	19	1,329	45,071	27,409	16,212

1. Karl has been Utah's leading scorer for many years. How many more points has he scored than Moses? *(Karl moved into second place on the all-time scoring list during the 2000–2001 season; the total points figure was at the start of that season.)*

_____

2. Moses was known as a powerful defender. He blocked shots and swallowed up rebounds. How many more rebounds does he have than Karl?

_____

3. When you examine his years in the league, Karl obviously plays more during each game. Using the statistics given, how many more minutes did Moses play?

_____

Reasoning questions

What is Karl's average minutes played per game? Knowing that he was still playing when this book was written, do you suppose Karl has passed Moses by now? Playing at his average minutes per game figure, how many games would Karl have to play in order to pass Moses in the total minutes played statistic?

_____

4. Moses scored a total of 27,409 points, which includes the record for most free throws made in a career. If he made 8,531 points on free-throws, how many points did he make on field goals?

_____

5. Karl Malone may break this record during the 2000–2001 season. Karl started the 2000 season with exactly 8,100 made free throws. How many free throws must he make to break the record?

_____

Foul play I

Every coach would like his or her team not to foul at all. A personal foul can send the opponent to the free-throw line for easy points. *(Coaches call the foul line the "charity stripe" for a reason.)* If a team doesn't foul the opponent, then the opponent doesn't get the "free" points. How good or bad have players been at following the coach's instructions of "Don't Foul!"

1. In 1983 Loyola of Maryland set the women's record for most fouls in a season. The team was called for 942 personal fouls in 27 games. What was its "fouls per game" average?

_____

2. The Boston University women's team holds the NCAA record for fewest fouls committed over a season. In 1987 the Boston U. women were called for only 261 fouls in 27 games. What was their "fouls per game" average?

_____

3. How many more fouls did the Loyola women commit, on the average per game, than the Boston U. women?

_____

4. Let's look at the men's figures. In 1987 the Providence College men's team was called for 966 fouls in 34 games. What was the team's "fouls per game" average?

_____

5. In 1962 the Air Force team was called for only 253 fouls in 23 games. What was its "fouls per game" average?

_____

6. How many more fouls did the Providence players commit, on the average per game, than the Air Force players?

_____

Foul play II

In high school and college basketball games, players are disqualified (sent to the bench for the rest of the game) when they receive their fifth foul. In the NBA, however, six fouls are required to send a player to the bench. Consider the NBA statistics contained in the following questions:

1. In 1976, Charlie Scott of Boston committed 35 fouls against Phoenix in a six-game postseason series. In how many games did Scott foul out?

_____

2. How close *(in terms of fouls)* did Scott come to fouling out in the next game?

_____

3. The record for most fouls in a seven-game series is 37. If a player commits this many fouls, what is the smallest possible number of times that he could foul out?

_____

Challenge problem

The record for most fouls in a three-game playoff series is 18. It is jointly held by Charlie Share of St. Louis (1956) and Vern Mikkelsen of Minneapolis (1957). Do these two old-time players need to worry about losing their records? Why or why not?

Sharing the ball

Every player likes to score but she or he has to get the ball first. This makes the person who passes the ball very popular with other players. Coaches also like a player who will distribute to another player who is open. If the open player makes a shot, the passer is credited with an assist.

Who were the leading assist players for the WNBA during the 2000 season?

Player	Team	Assists per game
Tichia Penicheiro	Sacramento	7.9
Teresa Weatherspoon	New York	6.4
Jennifer Azzi	Utah	6.1
Dawn Staley	Charlotte	5.9
Shannon Johnson	Orlando	5.3
Andrea Nagy	Washington	5.1
Cynthia Cooper	Houston	5.0

1. Figure that each assist resulted in a two-point basket. How many points did each of the players help earn for her team per game? *(Carry your answer out to one decimal point.)*

_____

2. What if each of the baskets was a three-point shot? How many points would each player help her team earn? *(Is this a logical assumption?)*

_____

Challenge problem

Since it is not probable that each assist will lead to a three-point basket, then the true number of points added by each player must be somewhere between answers one and two. Assume that each of the players had two assists that resulted in a three-point basket. How many points would they have assisted with?

I don't do windows

Rebounding in the WNBA is just as important as it is for the men of the NBA. Who were the rebounding leaders in 2000 for the WNBA? *(The figures in the table below are average rebounds per game for the 2000 WNBA season.)*

Player	Team	Offensive	Defensive	Total
Natalie Williams	Utah	4.6	7.0	11.6
Yolanda Griffith	Sacramento	4.6	5.7	10.3
Lisa Leslie	Los Angeles	2.3	7.2	9.6
Tari Phillips	New York	2.8	5.2	8.0
Tina Thompson	Houston	2.1	5.5	7.7

1. Can you compute the average number of offensive rebounds and the average number of defensive rebounds for these five players? Which is higher? Why do you think this is the case?

_____

2. Offensive rebounds usually result in more points for your team. This is because an offensive rebounder is usually in position to take a high percentage shot. If each offensive rebound resulted in two points for the team, figure how many extra points each player contributed to her team.

_____

3. Defensive rebounds usually prevent the other team from getting another shot. Therefore, if each defensive rebound prevented a two point basket, how many points did each player keep the other team from scoring?

_____

Division by I, II, and III

One of the best things about college basketball is its popularity. Almost all colleges have a basketball team. Basketball is played at big colleges, medium-sized colleges, and very small colleges. The NCAA has three divisions, based on size, in which colleges can compete. Championships are held in Divisions I, II, and III for both men and women. Records are kept for all three divisions. Consider the following records for most points in a game by a player playing against an opponent from the same division.

Year	Division	Player	School	Points
Men				
1954	II	Clarence "Bevo" Francis	Rio Grande	113
1991	I	Kevin Bradshaw	U.S. Int.	72
1988	III	Joe DeRoche	Thomas	63
Women				
1991	II	Jacki Givens	Ft. Valley State	67
1991	III	Ann Gilbert	Oberlin	61
1987	I	Cindi Brown	Long Beach State	60

1. How many points were scored, altogether, for the highest one-game men's totals? For the highest one-game women's totals? For both?

_____   _____

_____   _____

2. What is the average for the highest scores for men and women in Division I? Division II? Division III? For all three divisions combined?

_____   _____

_____   _____

3. "Bevo" Francis of Rio Grande is an interesting individual. He not only had the highest ever game score in Division II with 113 points, but he also had the second-highest game score, with 84 points, and the third-highest game score, with 82 points— all during the 1954 season. In addition, during the 1953 season, he tied for the seventh highest all-time game score with 72 points. In 1954 Francis averaged 46.5 points per game for 27 games. How many points did he score during that season?

_____

On the glass

During the playoffs, teams put extra effort into their defense. As a result, rebounding becomes very important during a playoff series. Records are kept for series that last from two to seven games.

1. The record for rebounds in a three-game playoff series is 84, held by Bill Russell of Boston. He set the record in 1957 against Syracuse. How many rebounds did Russell average per game?

_____

2. The second-best effort for rebounding in a three-game playoff is 69. Wilt Chamberlain recorded this total in 1961. How many more rebounds per game did Russell have than Chamberlain?

_____

Challenge problem

Since the 1973–74 season, rebounds have been broken down into two categories: offensive and defensive. The record for offensive rebounds in a three-game series is 28, set by Moses Malone in 1982. The record for defensive rebounds is 43, set by Bob McAdoo in 1976. By comparing these records, is it possible that one of the new records would belong to Russell if offensive and defensive rebound totals had been counted in 1957? Is it possible that both records could belong to Russell?

Chairman of the boards

The chart below shows rebounding records for a five-game playoff series.

	Player	Rebounds per game	Total rebounds
Total rebounds	Wilt Chamberlain—1967	32.0	
Offensive rebounds	Larry Smith—1987	7.2	
Defensive rebounds	Jack Sikma—1979	12.4	
	Karl Malone—1991	12.4	

1. Calculate the total rebounds for all four players on the chart above.

_____

2. How many defensive rebounds would Smith need to tie Chamberlain's mark?

_____

3. How many offensive rebounds would Malone need to tie Chamberlain's record for total boards?

_____

Challenge problem

During the 1978–79 season, 77% of Sikma's rebounds were on the defensive glass. If this pattern held true in the playoffs, how many offensive boards did he pull down? *(Round your answer to the nearest whole number.)*

REBOUNDING WINNER

Where's the offense?

On November 22, 1950, the Fort Wayne Pistons played the Minneapolis Lakers. The final score was Pistons 19, Lakers 18. It was the lowest scoring game in NBA history. Fort Wayne stalled most of the game to neutralize the Laker's height advantage. The league soon introduced the 24-second shot clock, eliminating stall tactics. The 24-second rule states that a team in possession of the ball must shoot within 24 seconds, or it loses the ball.

1. The Pistons made 4 of their 13 shots from the field for a 31% average. How many points did they score from the free-throw line? *(Remember that there was no three-point shot in 1950.)*

_____

2. If the Pistons missed four foul shots, how many total free throws did they attempt as a team?

_____

3. The Lakers hit 10 of 17 from the charity stripe. How many field goals did they make?

_____

4. Laker George Mikan scored five-sixths of his team's points. With how many points did he finish the game?

_____

5. Mikan scored all of his team's field goals. He also missed as many shots as the rest of the Lakers combined. If Minneapolis attempted 18 shots, how many did Mikan miss?

_____

6. John Oldham, a guard, led the Pistons with exactly one-third of Mikan's total number of points. How many points did this "high scorer" get?

_____

7. At the end of three quarters, the score was Pistons 16, Lakers 17. How many points did each team score in the final period?

_____

8. The length of the game was 48 minutes. Did the 7,021 fans get to see an average of at least one point scored per minute?

_____

9. The lowest scoring game after the introduction of the shot clock resulted in a Boston victory over Milwaukee, 62–57. How many more points were scored in this game than in the Pistons–Lakers match-up?

_____

Where's the defense?

The highest scoring game in NBA history took place on December 13, 1983, with the Denver Nuggets hosting the Detroit Pistons. The 1983 Pistons were nothing like the 1950 Fort Wayne Pistons, scoring 186 points to the Nuggets' 184. The game took three overtime periods to complete; six players from each team scored in double figures.

1. Detroit guards Isiah Thomas and John Long led the Pistons with 47 and 41 points, respectively. Did this duo score at least half of the Pistons' points?

2. Kiki Vandeweghe and Alex English led the Nuggets in scoring with 51 and 47 points, respectively. Did these two forwards account for half or more of the Denver total?

3. At the end of regulation playing time, the teams were tied at 135. How many points did Denver score in the three overtime periods? Detroit?

4. Although the teams combined for 370 points, only two three-point shots were made during the entire contest. If the teams combined for 84 points from the free-throw line, how many two-point field goals were made in the game?

5. Given that the two teams combined to make 84 free throws, and Denver made 10 more foul shots than Detroit, how many free throws did Denver convert? Detroit?

6. Including the three five-minute overtime periods, how many minutes of playing time did it take to declare a winner? *(Remember, pro games are 48 minutes long.)*

7. If the game took 3 hours and 11 minutes to complete, how much time was spent waiting for the action to resume?

8. Did the teams combine for an average of more than five points per minute?

9. On any other night, Detroit forward Kelly Tripucka's 35 points might have led the team. He scored four-fifths of his points on field goals. How many points did Tripucka have from the foul line?

Wilt's big night

On the night of March 2, 1962, the Philadelphia Warriors played the New York Knicks in Hershey, Pennsylvania. The star of the Warriors was Wilt "the Stilt" Chamberlain. Chamberlain had a reputation as a big scorer, but on this night he surpassed even his own high standards. He played every minute of the Warriors' 169 to 147 victory over the Knicks; at the end of the game, he had scored exactly 100 points. Chamberlain's quarter-by-quarter scoring appears below.

Quarters	1st	2nd	3rd	4th
Points	23	18	28	31

1. How many points did Chamberlain score in the first half of the game? the second half?

_____

_____

2. What was the difference between Wilt's best and worst quarter scores?

_____

3. How many points did the rest of the Warrior team combine to score?

_____

4. Chamberlain scored 72 points from the field. How many points did he score from the free-throw line?

_____

Defending the big guy

On the night Wilt Chamberlain scored 100 points for the Philadelphia Warriors, the New York Knicks also had a big offensive night. They scored 147 points, but they just couldn't stop the Warriors' big man. The Knicks box score is shown below.

Player	Field-goal attempts	Field goals made	Free-throw attempts	Free throws made	Points
Naulls	22	9	15	13	31
Green	7	3	0	0	6
Imhoff	7	3	1	1	7
Guerin	29	13	17	13	39
Butler	13	4	0	0	8
Buckner	26	16	1	1	33
Budd	8	6	1	1	13
Butcher	6	3	6	4	10

1. Darall Imhoff was the center for the Knicks. How many fewer points did he score than Chamberlain?

_____

2. Did the three top scorers for the Knicks—Naulls, Guerin, and Buckner—surpass Chamberlain's total?

_____

3. How many points did the Knicks "B-team" score? *(The "B-team" comprises all of the players whose last name starts with the letter B.)*

_____

Double-doubles

Ethan and Angela both play basketball for the Tigers. After an
away game, they compared their statistics on the bus ride home.
No one had totaled up the stats, so they had to do the job
themselves. Both players had done well in their games and each
was interested to see if they earned a double-double. When a
player reaches 10 in one statistic, he or she is said to have
reached double figures. A double-double is scored when a player
has reached double figures in two different statistical categories.
Ethan's stats are shown below.

Quarter	Points	Rebounds	Assists	Blocks	Steals
1	4	3	1	2	0
2	4	2	0	0	1
3	5	1	3	1	1
4	2	4	2	1	0

1. The players added up Ethan's numbers. Did Ethan reach a
double-double? In which statistical categories did he do the best?

Here are Angela's stats for her game.

Quarter	Points	Rebounds	Assists	Blocks	Steals
1	2	3	1	0	5
2	3	2	4	0	3
3	1	0	4	1	0
4	0	4	2	0	3

2. After Angela added up her points,
she began to think she missed a
double-double. Did she reach her goal
in this game? What were her best
categories?

Challenge problem

Try to make an educated guess about
what positions Angela and Ethan play.

_____

_____

Triple-doubles

After their teams finished beating their arch-rivals, the two coaches called the scores and statistics in to the newspaper. Gracie had been the star of the girls' game while Cory had played well for the boys' team. The stats for each player are listed below.

Gracie

Quarter	Points	Rebounds	Assists	Blocks	Steals
1	4	5	1	1	2
2	6	4	7	2	1
3	12	3	3	4	3
4	7	4	3	0	2

Cory

Quarter	Points	Rebounds	Assists	Blocks	Steals
1	10	8	1	2	3
2	4	4	2	0	5
3	7	5	6	3	0
4	11	4	0	4	3

1. Did either player have a triple-double or a double-double? If yes, in which statistical categories did they reach double figures?

_____

_____

2. Did Gracie miss reaching double figures in a category by just one? Did she miss any categories by two?

_____

_____

3. If every assist that Gracie and Cory had led to a two-point basket, how many points did the pair score or create via the assist?

_____

Challenge problem

Cory had a monster scoring night in the low post. From the stats provided, can you tell if Cory had a good game defensively?

Drawing the crowd

During the regular season, each NBA team is seen by lots of fans. Some of these games are so important or interesting that they are moved to larger stadiums. Domed football stadiums such as the old Kingdome in Seattle used to be used for these "big games."

1. The biggest crowd ever to see a regular season game was the 61,983 that packed the Silverdome to watch Boston play Detroit in 1988. Average attendance in Detroit's home court was 21,454 *(in 1992–93)*. How many more fans were able to see the game held in the Silverdome?

_____

2. If the Pistons had been able to pack the Silverdome all season long, what would their home attendance have been? *(Remember, each team has 41 home games.)* Use your calculator to find the answer.

_____

3. Some teams have smaller stadiums that sell out for every game. Portland, for example, has had a streak of sellouts for some time. The Trailblazers' total attendance in the 1992–93 season was 528,408. If every game was sold out, how many fans attended each game?

_____

Keeping time

The NBA has kept track of the number of games and minutes played since 1951. Many interesting times have been recorded since then. *(Remember that a game = 48 minutes.)*

1. In the 1961–62 season, Wilt Chamberlain played 3,882 minutes in 80 games. What is unusual about this statistic?

_____

2. The record for most minutes played in one game belongs to Dale Ellis. He played 69 minutes for Seattle in 1989. What would be the smallest number of overtime periods possible in this game? *(Overtime=5 minutes.)*

_____

3. Kareem Abdul-Jabbar holds the record for most minutes played in a career. He played 57,446 minutes in his 20 seasons with the Milwaukee Bucs and the Los Angeles Lakers. How many days are equal to 57,446 minutes? Use your calculator to find the answer.

_____

Challenge problem

In the 1968–69 season, Walt Bellamy played for New York and Detroit. Both of these teams played a regular 82-game schedule, yet Bellamy played in 88 games. This number, 88, is still the record for most games in one season. How could Bellamy have racked up this many games?

4. Randy Smith holds the record for the most consecutive games played, with 906. Assuming there are 82 games in a season, how many seasons did this iron man play without missing a single game?

_____

NBA trivia

Sports trivia can be fun. All you have to know are a few isolated facts that not very many other people know, and you can stump all of your friends. Here are a few examples of trivia brainteasers.

1. In the 1994–95 season, Toronto got a new NBA team, the Raptors. Is this the first Canadian team in the NBA?

2. What current team traces its roots to the Rochester Royals of 1948–49?

3. How many teams in the current Pacific Division (*Golden State, L.A. Clippers, L.A. Lakers, Phoenix, Portland, Sacramento, and Seattle*) have won an NBA title in their franchise history?

4. Which team has the record for the most wins in the regular season?

5. What was the original name and location of the Washington Wizards? What was their new nickname the next year? What was their new city and name for the team's third season?

Challenge problem

Find a basketball information book and make up trivia questions of your own.

Snack break

During the basketball season, each class in Hoopston High School sold food to raise money. The seniors sold hot dogs and pop. The juniors sold sandwiches and coffee. The sophomores brought cakes and cookies to sell. The freshmen sold candy. To save paper, the classes put all their prices on one big poster. The prices are shown below.

Hot Dogs	$1.00
Pop	.50
Sandwiches	1.75
Coffee	.50
Cakes	3.50
Cookies	.25
Candy	.50

At the end of one evening, in which both the boys' and girls' teams won big, the classes counted up their sales. The following chart shows the quantity sold of each item.

Cakes	11
Candy	48
Coffee	31
Cookies	98
Hot Dogs	76
Pop	119
Sandwiches	52

1. How much did each class make selling food at the basketball game?

2. What were the total sales?

The pep band blues

Solve the following problems.

1. The entire high school band cannot play at Killian High's home games. *(Two hundred fourteen musicians in a small gym would make too much noise!)* So, the pep band plays. If the pep band is made up of 27 musicians from the school band, how many school band members don't get to play at the basketball games?

2. When the band members take a break, they almost always buy a drink because their lips get so dry playing all those pep songs. If all 27 band members buy a lemonade for $1.25, how much do their refreshments cost?

3. Melinda, the band property officer, has to make small copies of the music to fit on the band members' instruments. If her counter says she made 486 reduced pages of music for the band, how many music sheets do each of the 27 players get?

Challenge problem

Kim, the lead trumpet player, has been in the pep band for three years. The team has 14 home games each season. If the pep band plays an average of 34 songs each night, how many songs has Kim played during her pep band career? Can you estimate how many times she has played "The Star Spangled Banner"? If so, how many?

Women's leading shooters

The following table shows the leading three-point shooters in women's college basketball.

 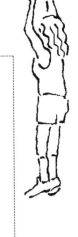

Player, Team	Last year	Years played	Games	Three-point field goals
Julie Krommenhoek, Utah	1998	4	117	362
Cornelia Gayden, LSU	1995	4	110	337
Karen Middleton, S. Carolina	1991	4	128	317
Jennifer Howard, NC State	1997	4	117	315
Kathy Halligan, Creighton	1992	4	115	309
Julie Jones, Richmond	1992	4	123	309

1. How many points did the record holder, Julie Krommenhoek, score on three-point plays? How many points did the other players listed score on their three-point baskets?

2. How many three-point baskets did Karen Middleton average during each of her games?

3. Are there players in the chart with more three-point baskets per game than Karen Middleton? If so, how many are there? List the players, if any, and the number of three-point baskets each averaged per game.

Challenge problems

Did you have to figure the average three-pointers per game for all of the other players, or could you figure out one that you did not have to compute the statistic for?

Accuracy counts

The preceding table on three-point shooters lists the total number of three-point shots made by the leading six women basketball long-distance shooters. But the percentage of shots made is also important. In the chart below, you will find five three-point shooters and their records of shots attempted and shots made.

Player, Team	Games	Three-point field goals	Three-pointers attempted	Percent
Karen Middleton, South Carolina	128	317	712	
Kathy Halligan, Creighton	115	309	680	
Julie Jones, Richmond	123	309	712	
Wendy Davis, Connecticut	127	279	635	
Kelly Savage, Toledo	92	273	708	

1. Before you start computing, can you predict whether Karen Middleton or Julie Jones will have the higher percentage-made figure? Why or why not?

_____

_____

2. Compute the percentage-made figures for each woman.

_____

_____

3. If the players were ranked by accuracy (the percentage-made figure), what would be the new order of players?

1. _____

2. _____

3. _____

4. _____

5. _____

Challenge problem

Which one of these players is no longer in the top 25 list of players with the highest three-point shooting percentages? Why?

PROJECTS

Interpreting box scores, LA Lakers

The Lakers box score for their win over Portland is shown below. This series was the most difficult for the Lakers to win on their route to the NBA championship in 2000. This was the seventh game, and the Lakers were behind going into the fourth quarter. But they outscored Portland 31 to 13 in the last quarter to come from behind and win.

Los Angeles Lakers

Player	Minutes	PTS	AST	REB	FGM	FGA	FTM	FTA	PF	ST	TO
Green	15	1	0	2	0	1	1	4	3	2	0
Rice	36	11	4	6	4	10	1	1	1	0	1
O'Neal	47	18	5	9	5	9	8	12	4	0	4
Bryant	47	25	7	11	9	19	6	12	4	0	2
Harper	23	9	4	2	4	6	1	2	3	0	1
Horry	33	12	0	7	4	7	3	6	4	0	2
Fisher	9	2	0	0	1	3	0	0	0	0	0
Fox	12	0	3	1	0	2	0	0	4	0	1
Shaw	17	11	2	3	4	6	0	0	2	2	2
Salley	1	0	0	0	0	0	0	0	0	0	0

1. The REB column lists each players' rebounding statistics. How many total rebounds did the Lakers get?

_____

2. The AST column lists the number of assists each player had. How many assists did the Lakers have on this night?

_____

3. The PTS column lists the total points scored by each player. If the Laker starters are shown by the positions they started (the letters in front of each player's name tell you who started at forward, center, and guard positions), then you can figure out how many points the starters had for the evening and how many points the reserves scored. (Those are usually described as "bench scoring" or "bench points.")

_____

4. Finally, the TO column lists turnovers. How many turnovers did the Lakers have on this night?

_____

Interpreting box scores, Portland Trailblazers

Look at the box score for the Portland Trailblazers in the seventh game of their playoff series with the Los Angeles Lakers in 2000. Then answer the questions below. Use your calculator to figure the answers.

Portland Trailblazers

Player	Minutes	PTS	AST	REB	FGM	FGA	FTM	FTA	PF	ST	TO
Pippen	46	12	3	10	3	10	4	4	6	2	3
Wallace	45	30	1	4	13	26	2	5	4	0	1
Sabonis	33	6	3	5	2	6	2	2	6	1	0
Smith	42	18	2	3	7	17	1	2	1	0	2
Stoudamire	20	5	3	1	2	6	0	0	2	1	0
Grant	8	0	1	2	0	2	0	0	2	0	1
O'Neal J	6	0	1	0	0	0	0	0	2	0	0
Wells	18	7	0	3	2	7	3	3	4	2	1
Schrempf	21	6	0	5	3	3	0	0	5	0	2
Anthony	4	0	1	0	0	0	0	0	0	0	0

1. Two important columns are the field-goal columns. For example, Scottie Pippen made three field goals and attempted ten. The FGM column lists field goals made; the FGA column lists field goals attempted. How many total field goals did Portland attempt in the game?

_____

2. The same idea applies to the free-throw columns. The FTM column lists free throws made and the FTA column lists how many were attempted. How many free throws did Portland make in the game?

_____

3. The percentage figures for made free throws and field goals are important. Find a Portland starter (the first five names on the list preceded by the letter for the position they play) who made a high percentage of his shots and one who did not.

_____

4. The PF column tells the number of personal fouls that each player had. If you have six personal fouls, you have to leave the game. Which player or players had the greatest number of personal fouls?

_____

Finding your team's box scores for a game

Now that you've seen what the information in the box score for a basketball game means, try doing the following:

1. Find the box score for your favorite basketball team. Can you identify what all the information means?

_____

2. Compare the box scores for a college team and a professional team. Do they provide the same information? Can you think of any information that might be found in your paper's box scores but not another's?

_____

3. Compare the winning team and the losing team. Who had more field goals? Who had more free throws? Who had more rebounds? Who had more offensive rebounds? Coaches often look at statistics such as these to help them figure out what their team is doing well—or not so well!

_____

_____

_____

4. What other interesting information about the game can you find reported in the box score?

_____

Charting shots

Coaches are concerned about where shots are taken and who takes them, so they do a shooting analysis as the game takes place. A basketball court diagram is placed on a clipboard. When a player shoots, the coach writes down the number of the player in the approximate position where the shot was taken. The coach circles the number if the shot is made. If the coach needs more room close to the basket, he or she makes other marks outside the court area, on the side where the shot was taken.

The diagram covers the first half of a game played by the Townville Tigers. Assume 5 players played, numbered 1 through 5; their shot record is shown on the chart.

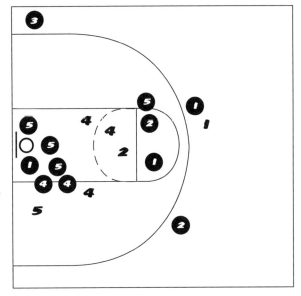

Center = number 5. This player took five shots, made four. The player made a long shot from near the free-throw line, and made three baskets close in; he or she missed one other shot close to the basket.

Forward = number 4. This player took five shots. He or she had three misses away from the basket, and made two shots close to the left side of the basket.

Forward = number 3. This player took/made one shot— a three-pointer from the right corner.

Describe the shots for these last two players.

Guard = number 2   Guard = number 1

Constructing a shooting chart

Watch a game on TV or better yet, go to a game in person and chart the shots. A blank chart is provided below. *(Refer to the instructions on the previous page as needed.)* After you have charted all the shots in a game, summarize your chart.

1. Figure statistics:

How many shots were taken?
How many shots were made?
How many shots did each player take?
How many shots did each player make?
Calculate the shooting percentage for the team and for each player.

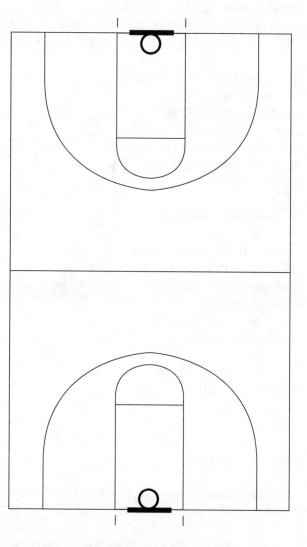

2. Examine the chart as a coach or player might examine it:

Did anyone take too many shots?
Who took shots from a place where he/she could not make them?
Who made almost all shots from a given area?
Did the team have enough "points in the paint" (meaning short, easy shots from inside the key)?
Did the team take very many three-pointers?
Who took three-point shots and made them? Missed them?

3. Make recommendations to the coach—for example:

"That forward can't make a shot more than five feet from the basket."

"That guard should not be shooting three-point shots. He missed them all."
"Pop that forward out for a long shot more often. She made them all."

Who is playing which position?

Over the last twenty years eveyone concerned with the NBA has begun to use numbers to describe the five positions on an ideal NBA basketball team. Those numbers and the positions they refer to are:

Number	Position	Duties
1	Point guard	Handle the ball and make assists Direct the team on offense
2	Shooting guard	Score, especially with three-point shots
3	Small forward	Score Run the floor on the fast break
4	Power forward	Rebound and play defense
5	Center	The Big Man—dominate the middle and also rebound and score
6	First sub	Come off the bench and give the team a lift

Coaches often talk about role players and how five people who play as a team win more games than five players striving for individual statistics. The best example of this ideal team was the Boston Celtics during the 1980s when Dennis Johnson was the 1, John Havelick the 2, Larry Bird the 3, Kevin McHale the 4, and Larry Parrish the 5. A role-playing substitute, Bill Walton, would come off the bench to substitute at both the 4 and 5 positions.

1. Examine the box scores of your favorite team. Determine who is playing which position. (Today's example: Gary Payton and John Stockton play the 1 position for Seattle and Utah, respectively, while Karl Malone is a 4 for the Jazz. Michael Jordan was a 2 for most of his career as are Reggie Miller and Kobe Bryant today. Shaq, of course, is a 5.)

2. After you have determined the position each player fills, keep statistics in order to check to see if each player fulfills the job's traditional role. Some players do, some players don't. At the point guard position, for example, John Stockton is the more traditional point guard while Allen Iverson is not.

Shooting treys

The three-point play was instituted to make the game of
basketball more interesting. A defensive team can choose to "clog
the lane" if it wants, but if all the defensive players are standing
in the lane, close to the basket, the offensive team has the
opportunity to shoot easy three-point baskets.

How does your favorite team use the three-point play?
Watch a game and answer the following questions.

1. How many three-point shots did your
favorite team attempt? How many did
the other team attempt?

_____

_____

2. How many of those three-point
attempts did your favorite team
make? How many did the other team
make?

_____

_____

3. Who scored the most points on three-
point shots?

_____

4. What happens if your favorite team
cannot make a three-point shot?
Does it change the defense that your
team faces?

_____

_____

Shooting from the charity stripe

Another vitally important statistic for a basketball team is the number of free-throw shots that it gets, and the number that it makes. To see just how important free throws really are, consider the following.

Some very good teams have lost championship games because they could not make free-throw shots. In the 1983 NCAA men's championship, for example, North Carolina State beat Houston. The University of Houston had an excellent team, including two future NBA all-stars: Houston's Hakeem Olajuwon and Portland's Clyde Drexler. But North Carolina State stole the championship game from the University of Houston because, at the end of the game, Houston could not make its free-throw shots. North Carolina State deliberately fouled Houston to get the ball back, and Houston could not convert those fouls into points.

Some teams seem to get a great many foul shots. Teams that shoot jump shots from a long distance never seem to get fouled, whereas those that drive to the basket always seem to get fouled. In the 1993 NCAA men's championship game, North Carolina beat Michigan. The Michigan team actually made more baskets than North Carolina, 30 to 27. But North Carolina made 18 of 23 free throws, while Michigan made only 6 of 7 free throws.

Using this information, answer the following questions:

1. Keep track of the foul shots for your favorite team during a game. How many foul shots did it get? How many foul shots did it make? What was the percentage of "made" shots? How many foul shots did the opponent get? How many did it make? What was the percentage of "made" shots?

_____

_____

_____

_____

2. You might also keep track of "crunch time" statistics. If your team was ahead with two or three minutes to play, were they fouled a lot at the end of the game? How many of those free throws did the team make?

_____

_____

3. Is there a reason why your favorite team is fouled often? Or, conversely, is there a reason why your team doesn't seem to get fouled often?

_____

_____

NBA defensive all-star team, 1999–2000

Many coaches value a player's defensive skills as well as, if not more than, the offensive skills. As a result, the NBA annually selects a defensive all-star team. These players are considered to be the best defensive players at their position. The positions, players, and the usual numbering system for the 1999–2000 season are shown here.

Number	Position	All-Star Player
1	Point guard	Gary Payton
2	Shooting guard	Kobe Bryant
3	Small forward	Kevin Garnett
4	Power forward	Tim Duncan
5	Center	Alonzo Mourning

Project

It is interesting to see the impact an all-star defender has on an opposing player. Does the all-star hold the opposing player to fewer points? Or, does he hold the opposing player to a lower shooting percenage? Or, does the all-star cause the opposing player to turn the ball over more often? Example: Allen Iverson was the leading scorer for Philadelphia in 1999–2000. But what happened when Philadelphia played Seattle? Did Gary Payton hold Allen to fewer points? Did Allen have a low percentage of shots made when playing against Gary? Or, did Allen turn the ball over more?

For a project, find the average points scored, shooting percentages, or turnovers in a game for a player. Then, when that player is defended by an all-star defender, check the game's box score to see what happened.

Remember, you must make certain which player the all-star defender was actually guarding. In the example given, it is logical to assume that Gary Payton would guard Allen Iverson, because they both play the point guard position. Similarly, it would be logical to assume that Karl Malone would be guarded by Tim Duncan, as they both play the power forward position. So, make certain you are checking the right player when you check statistics to see the impact of the all-star defender.

(A caution: Players often rest for some of each game. The all-star defender may not be guarding the other player every moment of the game. To use the example, see how many points Allen Iverson scored when Gary Payton was actually defending against him; omit the points Allen scored when Payton was on the bench.)

Comparing players

You can learn how to figure the "points per possession" statistic for a team. It might be interesting to see if individual players help or hurt their team's points per possession statistic.

1. The points are easy to find.

2. The possessions are not. You can calculate the number of possessions by adding the number of shots taken (both regular and three-pointers), the number of turnovers, and the number of foul shots that did not come after a made basket. *(This last number can be hard to find; you may have to estimate the number of possessions that ended in free throws by dividing the free-throw attempts by 2.)*

3. An individual player's points per possession, then, would be figured the same way as above. First, how many points did that player score? Second, how many possessions ended with this player handling the ball? You can estimate this by adding:

      a. The number of shots attempted.
      b. The number of turnovers.
      c. The number of free-throw attempts divided by 2.

Third, divide the number of possessions into the number of points scored to find the average points per possession.

4. In the paper find a box score for your favorite team. Calculate the points per possession for your team. Then, calculate the same statistic for one or more players. Did the player help the points per possession statistic by having a higher figure than the team, or did the player lower the points per possession statistic by having a lower figure than the team?

Keeping track of the defense

Watch a basketball game on television or go to a game in person. Keep defensive statistics on your favorite team. You might want to use the following chart. It has room for 12 players.

Player	Position	Steals	Blocks	Turnovers forced	Defensive rebounds

See if you find a pattern that allows you to answer these questions.

1. Which position or positions is *(are)* more likely to have blocked shots?

_____

2. Which position or positions is *(are)* more likely to have steals?

_____

3. Who is more likely to force a turnover?

_____

4. Who is more likely to get a defensive rebound?

_____

Keeping score for your favorite team

Watch a basketball game on TV or go to one in person. While you watch, keep score for your favorite team. You might want to use the following chart. It has 7 categories for you to fill in.

Use tally marks in each category as you watch; summarize them when the game is over.

Number	Name	Field goals		Free throws		Rebounds		Assists	Fouls
		Made	Attempted	Made	Attempted	Off	Def		

Keeping score for a game

Of course, keeping score for one team is only half of the task. You need to keep score for both teams. Here's how you can do it.

Watch a basketball game on TV with a friend. Use two scorecards similar to the one provided on the previous page. You keep score for one team and your friend can keep score for the other team.

Summarize your results after the game to find total points scored by each player, total rebounds, and related information. Then check the paper for the next day's box score to compare your scorekeeping with the official scorekeeper's record.

Women's basketball before the NCAA

All women's basketball records included in this book come from the NCAA, the National Collegiate Athletic Association. Official NCAA women's basketball records began with the 1981–82 season, the season in which the NCAA took over women's college sports. Changes in the law that occurred about that time required that colleges spend more money on women's athletics—in an effort to make these equivalent to men's athletic programs.

This does not mean, however, that women's basketball began in 1981. Nothing could be further from the truth. An active women's basketball program existed before that time. It organized national championships and named All-American teams, among other things.

Go to the library and look up information on women's basketball prior to 1981. Read through old newspapers and magazines to see what you can find. Women's sports were not widely publicized; even so, there were some famous players, in addition to a women's professional basketball league and women's Olympic basketball championships. Your research will turn up some interesting stories about women athletes who did not get the fame or fortune they deserved.

Keeping team statistics

One of the most interesting projects you can undertake is to keep the season's statistics for your favorite team, whether that team is a high school team, a college team, or a professional team. You can get the information you need from the box scores for each game printed in your local newspaper. You can often check your statistics against the newspaper's statistics by finding out what day of each week the newspaper publishes its totals for the season to date.

What statistics should you keep? Consider the following list.

1. Scores for each game.

What was the average margin of victory for your team? (Average all your team's winning scores, average all the other teams' losing scores, and subtract to find the average difference. This is the average margin of victory.)

What was the average margin of defeat for your team?

How many more points did your team score when it won?

2. Number of field goals attempted—for both your team and the opponent.

3. Number of field goals made—for both your team and the opponent. Average these figures to find out:

Who shot more—your favorite team or the other team?

Who made more shots?

Who had the best shooting percentage?

Were these figures different in the wins and losses?

Continue by answering the four questions in problem 3 for the following categories:

4. Number of free throws attempted— for both teams.

_____   _____

_____   _____

5. Number of free throws made—for both teams.

_____   _____

_____   _____

Keeping player statistics

Another interesting season-long project is to keep statistics on your favorite player or players. Again, you can find the information you need in your daily newspaper; add up the figures to get the season-long statistics.

What statistics should you keep? Consider the following list:

1. Number of points in each game. Average to find the number of points per game. Average to find the number of points in winning and losing games. Is there a difference? Does your team win when your favorite player has a good night and lose when he or she has a bad one?

2. Number of free throws in a game. Consider the number made and the number shot. Is your favorite player a good free-throw shooter? Examine the following table to help you decide:

Making 90%—Outstanding; record performance.

Making 80% to 90%—Excellent free-throw shooter.

Making 70% to 80%—Good free-throw shooter.

Making 60% to 70%—Okay, but really not very good.

Making 60% or less: We need to work on this!!!

3. Number of field goals in a game. Again, consider the number made and the number shot. Is your favorite player an accurate shooter? Anything over 40% is okay in high school or college; professionals should do better than that. Anything over 50% is excellent for anyone. Remember that distance is often a factor; centers usually have better shooting percentages than guards.

4. Number of rebounds, steals, blocked shots, and so on. Consider your favorite player's position. If he or she is a guard, then you would expect fewer rebounds. If he or she is a center, you would expect more rebounds and blocked shots. Guards might have more steals than a center or a forward.

Second-chance points

Rebounding is one of the keys to a winning basketball team. A team that protects the defensive boards *(by rebounding most of the opponent's missed shots)* prevents that opponent from getting second and third chances to score. Similarly, a team that gets offensive rebounds *(getting the rebound after its own missed shots)* has those second and third chances to score. When watching basketball games on TV, you will often see reports on second-chance points. Second chance points are those points scored by your team *(or the opposing team)* after first missing a shot.

You can keep and interpret statistics on rebounding that will tell you about second-chance point possibilities. Consider the following:

1. A team took 80 shots. The team made 40 of those shots.

With this information, you can figure the shooting percentage. The team shot 50%. That is excellent; you will win most games by shooting 50%.

2. Say you also know that the team collected 15 offensive rebounds. That probably means it got 15 "second-chance shots." If so, the team actually had the ball 65 times. It made a basket 40 of those times. You can figure this percentage. It's much higher than your answer to number 1, isn't it? What can we learn from this? If your team collects offensive rebounds, it will score more points.

Collect offensive rebounding statistics for your favorite team over the course of a year. You might even want to collect offensive rebounding statistics for a good team *(one with a winning record)* and a poor team *(one with a losing record).*

There is an excellent chance that the number of offensive rebounds will be greater for the winning team. Good luck with your research.

Being offensive

It is interesting to see which players are good offensive rebounders. Some players collect large numbers of rebounds, but very few are offensive rebounds; others, such as Dennis Rodman, work hard to get offensive rebounds. Let's create a "being offensive" rebounding statistic.

Consider the following situation: Sally plays for the Cougars. She gets 14 rebounds in a game. Four of these are offensive rebounds. What percent of Sally's rebounds are offensive rebounds?

To answer the question, divide the number of offensive rebounds by the total number of rebounds. This gives you the "being offensive" statistic:
4/14 = 28%

Thus, 28% of Sally's rebounds were offensive rebounds.

Using this statistic, along with the actual number of offensive rebounds can help you judge a player's ability to help his or her team with offensive rebounds.

Collect rebounding statistics for several players and then compute the "being offensive" statistic for them. Which of your players has the best percentage?

A statistic is worth more when it is collected over several games. Anyone can have a good or a bad night. But if you collect the rebounding figures for several games, you will have a statistic that gives you better information about your favorite players.

Clutch time free throws

Consider the following situation: The game is close. Your team is ahead by three points. There are only 15 seconds left. Your team has the ball. What will happen next?

Everyone knows the answer: your opponent will try to foul your worst free-throw shooter. Maybe he or she will miss; the opposing team will get the ball back, and it will try to tie the score.

It's called "clutch time." Players have to make their free throws at the end of a game, in the "clutch," to protect the lead. Are they good at it? You can figure that out.

1. Watch your favorite team on TV or go to a local game. You can find a player's free-throw shooting percentage in the paper, or they are often shown on TV as well. Once you have this number, do the following:

Wait until the last three minutes of a game. Then record:
> The number of foul shots each player gets.

> Whether it is a "one and one" or not.

> How many shots each player makes.

Then, figure out the free-throw percentage for "clutch time."

2. Which players shot better (than their regular free-throw percentage) at the end of the game? Which ones shot worse? Repeat this process for several games. What did you find?

3. Pretend you are the coach. If you were protecting a small lead, which players would you want in the game during the last few minutes?

Are teams getting taller?

As women's basketball becomes more popular, coaches are finding and training taller women to be basketball players. Many women's basketball teams now have players who are 6 feet 2 inches tall or taller. At one time UCLA's men's basketball team, the men's national champions, played a 6-foot-1-inch forward. Today, you would never see a forward that "short" on a men's team, and you would find that most women's teams have players taller than that starting at forward and center.

How tall are the women's teams getting to be? Why don't you start a season-long project to find out?

1. Check to see when women's basketball games are broadcast in your area. Look for a local sports network on cable *(Pacific Northwest Sports, Sunshine Network, etc.)*. Or, look in your TV guide for any national or regional games that might be on one of the major networks. Or, finally, see if you can find local broadcasts of your area's college teams.

2. Watch the first five minutes of the program, when the sportscasters announce the starting lineups. Usually, at that time the player's vital statistics *(height, position, scoring average, etc.)* are also given.

3. Keep a journal in which you record the tallest players for each team. See how many women players you can find who are 6 feet 2 inches or taller. After you are done collecting data, you might convert all the heights to inches and graph the tallest players by team. You might even compare the graphs from one season to the next. Are teams getting taller?

Average heights

Basketball players come in all sizes. In the NBA Mugsy Boges is only 5 feet 3 inches tall. By contrast, Shawn Bradley is 7 feet 6 inches tall. That is a difference of 2 feet 3 inches. There have even been NBA players who were taller than 7 feet 6 inches.

We often talk about how the "average height" of the players is getting taller. What does "average height" mean? If you add all the players' heights together, and divide by the number of players, you get the average height for a team. At one time, only 25 years ago, teams might have an average size of only 6 feet 3 inches. Now, most professional teams are much larger than that, most college teams are much larger, and even many high school teams have a much larger starting lineup.

1. Locate the height information for your favorite team. It will be published in your newspaper; you might also find it in a basketball magazine or on the Internet.

2. Find the average height for your team. (*You might even want to figure out the average height for the starting five players and then for the entire team.*) Then find the average height for all of the teams in your league.

3. Who are the short teams and who are the tall teams in your league? Who wins the most games, the tall teams or the short teams? Who scores the most points, taller or shorter players? Why?

4. Has the three-point rule helped make shorter players more important in basketball?

Being defensive

As in almost every sport, the basketball team that plays better defense is the team that is more likely to win. Scoring may be spectacular, but defense is what wins the game. Here are the four major defensive statistics in basketball that show how the defensive team is doing.

Defensive Rebounding: One of the most important aspects of playing defense is making certain that your opponent only gets one shot at the basket. If the opposing team misses, your team must rebound to prevent second-chance points.

Steals: If one of your players can steal the ball from an opposing player, then he or she can't score because you have the ball.

Blocked Shots: Again, if one of your players can block the opponent's shot, then the ball can't go in the basket and the opponent can't score.

Turnovers: If you can steal the ball, intercept a pass, or force the other team to lose the ball out of bounds, you have again prevented the opposing team from scoring.

Keep defensive statistics on your favorite team for a game or for a season. Or, compare two teams. Which one has the better defensive statistics? If you're comparing two teams that are actually playing one another, there is an excellent chance that the one with the better defensive statistics is the winning team.

Point differential

Point differential is a statistic used to rate the overall success of basketball teams. Some teams like to play up tempo, fast break basketball with lots of scoring. Other teams like to slow the tempo of a game and concentrate on defense. Since teams use different philosophies, studying offensive or defensive statistics alone cannot tell you everything about a team's performance.

Point differential is found by subtracting the average number of the opponent's points from your team's average number of points. Chicago's +6.3, for example, means that the Bulls scored an average of 6.3 more points per game than their opponents throughout the season. Use the chart to answer the following questions.

1992-93			
	Average points scored	Average points allowed	Point differential
Chicago	105.2	98.9	+6.3
Phoenix	113.4	106.7	
Charlotte		110.4	−0.3
L.A. Clippers	107.1		+0.3
New York	101.6	95.4	
Dallas	99.3	114.5	
Seattle	108.5	101.3	

1. What was the point differential for Phoenix?

_____

2. Charlotte's point differential was −0.3. What was the team's average number of points scored per game?

_____

3. The Clippers scored an average of 107.1 points per game and had a positive point differential of 0.3. Did they average more or fewer points than their opponents? How many points did their average opponent score?

_____

Fill in the blanks on the chart on page 82 and use the completed table to answer the questions below.

4. Four of the teams listed in the chart advanced to the conference finals in the 1993 playoffs. Judging from the point differential statistic, which four teams would you guess made it to the finals?

_____

_____

_____

_____

5. Which of the listed teams would you pick as most likely to have missed the playoffs entirely?

_____

_____

_____

6. The Clippers had a point differential of +0.3 and finished the regular season with exactly the same number of wins and losses, 41 of each. Charlotte had a point differential of −0.3, yet finished the season at 44–38.

What could account for a Hornets' winning record but negative point differential?

_____

_____

_____

7. The four teams with the highest point differential in the chart all finished among the top five teams in the league in this category. See if you can find out which team that is not listed in the chart also finished in the top five in point differential.

_____

8. Calculate the point differential for your favorite team for one week or, better yet, for one month.

_____

_____

Who's my nemesis?

Some teams seem to play particularly well against other teams. From 1991 to 1993, for example, the Chicago Bulls won three straight championships but had identical 1–5 records against San Antonio and Houston. Chicago never faced those teams in the playoffs, but if the regular season records were any indication, they might have had trouble.

In the 1993–94 regular season, Seattle had the best record in the NBA but was only 2–2 against Denver. In the same year, Utah went 5–0 against San Antonio even though the Spurs had a better record overall. In both cases, the team with the better record lost to the underdog during the playoffs.

In recent years, the New York Knicks have been the Miami Heat's nemesis. New York eliminated Miami from the playoffs in three consecutive seasons—1997–1998, 1998–1999, and 1999–2000. This was true, even though in all three of those seasons, Miami won the Eastern Division title. In fact, Miami was the top-ranked team in the Eastern Conference one year, and New York was the eighth-ranked team. So, despite the fact that New York barely made it into the playoffs, they still proved they were Miami's nemesis!

Keep track of your favorite team's records against the rest of the league. If you record the results of each night's game on a chart, by playoff time you will know the results of the season series between your team and any other team in the league.

Can you play defense?

Sometimes a basketball player will get a reputation for scoring a lot of points but not playing any defense. On a good night, such a player might score 28 points, while the man that he guards scores only 15. The coach will look at the box score the next day and be pleased that the player scored +13. On a bad day, the same player might score 20 points but give up 35 points. When the coach sees that the player allowed 15 more points than he scored, the player might see more time on the bench.

Before a game, choose a player who has a reputation for scoring a lot of points. Keep track of how many points that player scores. Also keep track of the point total for any player he guards. At the end of the game, decide whether the player works well at both ends of the court or is primarily a scorer.

You might also look to see which player the high scorer is guarding. Is it the other team's leading scorer? Sometimes a coach will try to "hide" a weak defender by having him cover a player who doesn't shoot the ball very often. If the low scorer has a big night, you will know that the high scorer is mostly an offensive player with "no D."

When are you "above average"?

It seems to make sense that a basketball star would have his or her best games against weaker competition. Some players, however, seem to do better against the best teams and the best players. This type of player is called a "big-game player."

One way to see whether a given player is a big-game player is to compare that player's statistics in the important games of the year to his or her yearly averages. For example, if Shaquille O'Neal is averaging 30 points per game during the season, see how he does against another star player. If Shaq must face another superstar, how does he do? Keep track of the points, rebounds, and blocks each of the two big men get. By comparing these numbers against the season averages, you can see whether one of the players rises to the occasion of the big game. Don't fall into the trap of generalizing from one game, however. Try to get records over several games to see who does best in the long run.

Keep a chart of your favorite player's statistics in games in which he or she plays against other big-name stars. If you find the average of these games and compare it to the seasonal average, you will get a good idea of how that player handles first-rate competition.

Backs against the wall

The NBA playoffs are a pressure cooker of excitement and tension. Coaches and teams worry about such things as home court advantage and adjustments made by the opposing team. Many teams go so far as to foul rather than allow an easy basket. The emotion can reach fever pitch.

When a playoff team is one game from elimination, it is said to have its back against the wall. That team will play as hard as it can since one loss will finish its season. Sometimes both teams are one loss from elimination. This only happens in the fifth game of a best-of-five series or the seventh game of a best-of-seven series. During these deciding games, the pressure goes through the roof. Watch a "backs against the wall" game and see who plays well and who does not, who scores a lot of points and who does not. In other words, see who plays well with his "back against the wall."

In the playoffs, wait for a deciding playoff game—one in which the winner advances and the loser goes home—to occur. After the game, look at the statistics for each player. Usually in a big game, one or two players will make big plays at the end of the game, while several others may have carried the team in the early or middle stages. These players are generally the unsung heroes unless they make some big plays late in the game. See if you can identify an unsung hero who plays best when his team has its back against the wall.

Charting the playoffs

Playoff chart

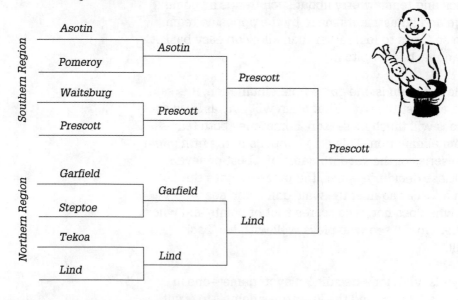

One of the things that makes basketball exciting is the playoffs. College basketball has "March Madness," where both men and women's teams are selected to play for the national championships. The NBA has an elaborate playoff system to determine its league champion. Even high schools in most states take part in playoffs to crown a state champion.

A sample playoff chart appears above. It records the eight high-school teams that started in the playoffs, located in two different brackets. Of the starting eight teams, four advanced to the second round because they won those first games. Of the four teams playing in the semifinal games, two advanced to the championship game, and of those two teams, only one won the championship. You can see here that the Prescott Tigers have won our mythical championship.

You will find the playoff charts in your local newspaper each spring when the college playoffs begin. Sixty-four teams are selected; 16 teams are assigned to each region. Cut out this beginning chart and record all of the winners. Or, if you prefer, make a chart for your own high-school team as it moves through the state championship. Alternatively, you might make a chart showing the NBA playoffs. Fashion your handmade charts after the one pictured above.

Answer key

Answers vary in activities for which answers are not provided below.

Creating a dynasty
1. Answers will vary; for 2001 it is 52 years. Add more as years change.
2. 505
3. 963; 5,909
4. 3,776

The post-season party
1. 40 games
2. 24 games
3. 4 games
4. 7 series
5. 49 games
6. 28 games
7. 89 games; 52 games

March madness
1. 33 games (including extra games)
2. 8 games; 16 teams
3. 6 rounds
Challenge problem: 9

Women's unbeaten teams
1. 2,853 points
2. 26.7 points per game
3. 141.1 points per game
4. 162 points
5. 34.2 field goals per game

Men's unbeaten teams
1. 323 games
2. 8 games
3. 120 wins
4. a. answer varies by year; b. answer varies by year

The Warriors, state champs
1. 274 points; 208 points
2. 68.5 points per game; 52 points per game
3. 24, 6, 28, and 8 points, respectively
4. 16.5 points per game

Women's scoring champions
1. 33.0 points per game
2. 31.0 points per game
3. 907 points
4. 326 more points
5.   Hoskins   28.4 points per game
       Bauman   26.0 points per game
       Holdsclaw 20.4 points per game

The Big "O"
1. 1,052 field goals
2. 2,973 points
3. 869 free throws
Challenge problem: He averaged 33.8 points per game. The team did not play the same number of games each season.

"Pistol" Pete
1. 1,387 field goals
2. 3,667 points
3. 893 free throws
Challenge problem: Answers will vary. Examples: field-goal percentage, shots per game, turnovers, etc.

Point guards
1. 2.25:1
2. 12 turnovers
3. 60 assists
4. 1.6:1
5. Efrain, who had the most assists and turnovers, started.

Women's field-goal percentage leaders

Larsen	1998	28	249	344	72.4
Knowles	1996	26	199	276	72.1
Farris	1998	27	151	210	71.9
Adams	1991	30	185	258	71.7
Days	1986	27	234	332	70.5
Woods	1994	27	188	271	69.4

Comparing field-goal percentages
1. 388 times
2. 776 points
3. 149 times
4. 298 points

Challenge problem: Player A's team made 0.9 points for every time she shot the ball. Player B's team made 1.3 points for every time she shot the ball.

UCLA's championships
1. 13 years
2. 10 first-place finishes
3. 2 third-place finishes
4. 1 time
5. 84.6 points per game
6. 71.2 points per game
7. 13.4 points per game

Duke's championships
1. 9 years
2. 2 first-place finishes
3. 3 second-place finishes
4. 2 times
5. 2 times
6. 71.4 points per game

NCAA women's championships
1. a. 78.5; b. 66.5; c. 12
2. a. Connecticut 70.5; Stanford 83
   b. Connecticut 54.5; Stanford 71.5
   c. Connecticut 16; Stanford 11.5
3. 16; 4.5
4. Texas Tech, Purdue, North Carolina

Sheryl Swoopes, 1993 MVP
1. 50.9%
2. 61 free throws
3. 9.6 rebounds per game
4. 35.4 points per game

Challenge problem: She made 8 three-point shots.

Hiding the three-point shots
Bauman 0
Swoopes 2
Holdsclaw 0
Bascom 1
Cate 1
Swoopes 1

Mom's challenge problems
1. 15 points
2. 14 field goals; 7 free throws
3. 70 points

Charity stripe stories
1. 95.80%
2. 45.60%=Shaq's playoff percentage for 2000 playoffs
3. 91.87%
4. 31.87%
5. 48.15% FTM for 1985–1986; 79.70% FTM for 1999–2000; 31.55% improvement

NBA record holders
All-time scoring leader
Points: 38,387
Years: 20
Points per year: 1,919.35

All-time playing leader
Kareem's minutes: 57,446; played 11,742 more minutes than Parrish

All-time shot leader
Shots made: 15,837
Shots attempted: 28,307
Shooting percentage: 55.95
Three-point shooting percentage: 5.56%

Hot shots
1. Anji does, with 16.1 points
2. Anji has
3. No, she is not.
4. 16.25 points per game
5. 24 points

Shooting for the perimeter
1. 288 feet
2. 50 feet
Challenge problems: Perimeter = 68.8 feet, circumference = 37.7 feet

Covering the area
1. 228 square feet; 456 square feet
2. 113.0 square feet
3. 56.5 square feet; 113.0 square feet
4. 4,700 square feet

Famous duos

1. Stockton
   Assists: 13,780
   Seasons: 16
   Average: 861.25

   Malone
   Points: 31,041
   Seasons: 15
   Average: 2,069.40

2. Duncan : 1, 084
   Robinson: 775
   Duncan scored 309 more points.

3. Pippin: 1,720
   Jordan: 2,580
   Total: 4,300 combined points

4. Larry: 2,295
   Magic: 1,909
   Difference: 386

The NBA all-star team, 1999–2000

1. First team's total=8,858
   Second team's total=9,193
   The second team scored more.

2. First Team:

	Garnett	Duncan	O'Neal	Payton	Kidd
Games	81	74	79	82	67
PPG	22.93	23.19	29.67	24.17	14.31

Second Team:

	Hill	Malone	Mourning	Iverson	Bryant
Games	74	82	79	70	66
PPG	25.76	25.55	21.75	28.41	22.50

Read and compute
Payton and Malone
Bryant

Misses

Garnett	1	Hill	8
Duncan	8	Malone	0
O'Neal	3	Mourning	3
Payton	0	Iverson	12
Kidd	15	Bryant	16

		Points	Average
3. Garnett	Hill	49.00	2.83
Duncan	Malone	379.00	2.36
O'Neal	Mourning	(626.00	7.92)
Payton	Iverson	7.00	4.24
Kidd	Bryant	526.00	8.19

All second teamers except Mourning outscored their counterparts. Greatest point difference: Second over First–Bryant over Kidd. Difference equals 526 points or 8.19 points per game.

Shot blockers

1. 262 total points or 8 points per game
2. 10.2 more points per game for the opposing team
3. 5.6 blocks per game
4. 137 shots

Wanted for stealing

1. a. 42; b. 28; c. 14
2. 191 season points prevented
Reasoning question: Yes. Seven steals had to result in fewer points for the other team.

Very famous players doing other things

1. 31.25%
2. Regular season winning percentage=68.7%
   Playoff winning percentage=61.5%
   Total winning percentage=67.3%
3. Lost games=25
   Total games=30
   Winning percentage=17%

Play like Mike

1. He scored 1,905 more points in his first year.
2. He averaged 25.06 minutes per game.
3. Highest=3,041; Lowest=408; Difference=2,633

Son of play like Mike

1. Mike's Points Year 1=2,313; Kobe's Points Year 1=539; Difference=1,774. Mike scored 1,774 more points in his rookie season.
2. Mike's Minutes Year 1=3,144; Kobe's Minutes Year 1=1,103; Difference=2,041. Mike played 2,041 more minutes in his first year.
Common sense questions: Kobe was not a starter as a rookie. Mike was injured during his second year.
3. Mike's Average=37.1; Kobe's Average=22.5; Difference=14.6. Mike averaged 14.6 more points.

Do you really want to hold this record?

Quickest disqualification ever: Bubba Wells would commit 96 fouls during the entire game.
All time leader in turnovers: Moses Malone had 200.21 turnovers on average per season.

Amazing championship stories

1. 207 points
2. 125 points

Three famous college shot blockers

1. 308 shots
2. 5.75 shots
3. 104 shots
Challenge problem: It would be impossible to have "record performances" over every game in a season.

Senator Bradley's records

1. 24 years
2. 46 attempts
Challenge problem: There might be many players who made 1 free throw and had only 1 attempt. This would be a "cheap" record.

The long and the short of it

1. Camby, Knight, Longley, Rice, Thomas
2. 414 inches
3. 379 inches
4. Longley to Ward=12 inches (range in height)
5. 216.8 pounds (total weight of all players – 2,602–divided by 12, the number of players)
6. Longley to Ward or Sprewell=70 pounds (range in weight)
7. Heaviest=1,185 pounds; Lightest=985 pounds
8. Yes, except Postell does not tie for this one.

All-time records

All-time steal leader: Stockton=2,844 steals
Who's doing it now? Payton=175.6 steals per year
All-time rebounding leader: Wilt=1,708.9 rebounds per year
Who's doing it now? Rodman averaged 853.9 rebounds per year, so Wilt had 855 more.
Calculator problem: Wilt=.49988 rebounds per minute; Rodman=.4141 rebounds per minute

Two famous Malones

1. Karl's Points: 31,041; Moses' Points: 27,409; Difference: 3,632. Karl had 3,632 more points by the beginning of the 2000–2001 season.
2. Moses' Rebounds: 16,212; Karl's Rebounds:12,618; Difference: 3,594. Moses had 3,594 more rebounds.
3. Moses' Minutes: 45,071; Karl's Minutes: 44,608; Difference: 463. Moses played 463 more minutes.
Reasoning questions: Karl plays 37.42 minutes per game; Karl should pass Moses in the 12th game of the 2000–2001 season
4. Moses scored 18,878 points of field goals.
5. Karl needs 432 more free throws to break Moses' record

Foul play I

1. 34.9 fouls per game
2. 9.7 fouls per game
3. 25.2 fouls per game
4. 28.4 fouls per game
5. 11 fouls per game
6. 17.4 fouls per game

Foul play II

1. 5 games
2. 1 foul
3. 2 times
Challenge problem: No, since 18 (6 fouls times 3 games) is the maximum number of fouls possible.

Sharing the ball

Player	1. Points earned	2. Points earned	Challenge problem
Penicheiro	15.8	23.7	17.8
Weatherspoon	12.8	19.2	14.8
Azzi	12.2	18.3	14.2
Staley	11.8	17.7	13.8
Johnson	10.6	15.9	12.6
Nagy	10.2	15.3	12.2
Cooper	10	15	12

I don't do windows

1. Offensive:

Offensive	Defensive
4.6	7
4.6	5.7
2.3	7.2
2.8	5.2
2.1	5.5
16.4	30.6
Average=3.28	Average=6.12

Defensive; it's easier to get a defensive rebound. You are between your opponent and the basket.

2.
Williams	4.6	2	9.2
Griffith	4.6	2	9.2
Leslie	2.3	2	4.6
Phillips	2.8	2	5.6
Thompson	2.1	2	4.2

3.
Williams	7	2	14
Griffith	5.7	2	11.4
Leslie	7.2	2	14.4
Phillips	5.2	2	10.4
Thompson	5.5	2	11

Division by I, II, and III

1. 248 points; 188 points; 436 points
2. I-66, II-90, III-62, combined = 72.7
3. 1,256 points

On the glass

1. 28 rebounds per game
2. 5 rebounds per game
Challenge problem: Yes, Russell had 13 more rebounds than MacAdoo and Malone combined. This makes it possible for him to have both records.

Chairman of the boards

1. 160 rebounds; 36 rebounds; 62 rebounds; 62 rebounds
2. 124 rebounds
3. 98 rebounds
Challenge problem: 16 boards

Where's the offense?

1. 11 points
2. 15 free throws
3. 4 field goals
4. 15 points
5. 7 shots
6. 5 points
7. Pistons 3, Lakers 1
8. No, they did not. (.8 points per minute)
9. 82 points

Where's the defense?

1. No, they did not.
2. Yes, they did.
3. Denver 49, Detroit 51
4. 140 field goals
5. Denver 47, Detroit 37
6. 63 minutes
7. 2 hours, 8 minutes
8. Yes, they did. 5.87 points per minute
9. 7 points

Wilt's big night

1. 41 points; 59 points
2. 13 points
3. 69 points
4. 28 points

Defending the big guy

1. 93
2. Yes, they did. 103 points
3. 64 points

Double-doubles

Ethan:
   Points 15, Rebounds 10,
   Assists 6, Blocks 4, Steals 2
1. Yes; points and rebounds
Angela:
   Points 6, Rebounds 9;
   Assists 11, Blocks 1, Steals 11
2. Yes; assists and steals
Challenge problem: Ethan—Center, Angela—Guard

Triple-doubles

Gracie:
  Points 29; Rebounds 16
  Assists 14, Blocks 7, Steals 8
Cory:
  Points 32, Rebounds 21
  Assists 9, Blocks 9, Steals 11

1. Yes, both players had a triple-double.
   Gracie—Points, rebounds, assists
   Cory—Points, rebounds, steals
2. No. Yes.
3. 46 points
Challenge problem: Yes. Lots of blocks/steals.

Drawing the crowd

1. 40,529
2. 2,541,303
3. 12,888

Keeping time

1. Chamberlain averaged more than 48 minutes per game, which is remarkable when one considers that 48 minutes is the length of a regular NBA game. Many of his games went into overtime.
2. 5 overtimes
3. 39.89 days
4. Just over 11 seasons
Challenge problem: When Bellamy was traded, his original team had played 6 more games than his new team.

NBA trivia

1. No, the Toronto Huskies played in 1946 and tied the Boston Celtics for last place in the Eastern Division.
2. the Sacramento Kings
3. 5 teams
   Golden State in 1975
   L.A. Lakers in 1972, 80, 82, 85, 87, 88
   (and as the Minneapolis Lakers in 1949, 50, 52,53)
   Portland in 1977
   Sacramento in 1951 (as the Rochester Royals)
   Seattle in 1979
4. L.A. Lakers, 1971–72, 69–13
5. a. Chicago Packers, 1961–62
   b. Chicago Zephyrs, 1962–63
   c. Baltimore Bullets, 1963–64

Snack break

1. Seniors $135.50
   Juniors $106.50
   Sophomores $63.00
   Freshmen $24.00
2. $329.00

The pep band blues

1. 187 members
2. $33.75
3. 18 sheets
Challenge problem: Kim has played 1,428 songs; Yes, 42 times.

Women's leading shooters

1. 1,086 points scored on three-point baskets for Julie; Cornelia=1,011; Karen=951; Jennifer=945; Kathy and Julie=927
2. 2.48 three-pointers
3. All five have a higher per-game average
   Averages for the other players are:
   Krommenhoek   3.09
   Gayden   3.06
   Howard   2.69
   Halligan   2.69
   Jones   2.51
Challenge problem: Discuss games played and three pointers made. How do the ties influence the answer?

Accuracy counts

1. Yes, Middleton will be higher. She made more shots in the same number of attempts.
2. Middleton   44.5%
   Halligan   45.4%
   Jones   43.4%
   Davis   43.9%
   Savage   38.6%
3. 1 Halligan
   2 Middleton
   3 Davis
   4 Jones
   5 Savage
Challenge problem: Savage, because she is at the bottom of the ordered list.